DEVILISH
DARLINGS
PORTAL
FANTASY
story and art by
Minoru Mitsuba

CONTENTS

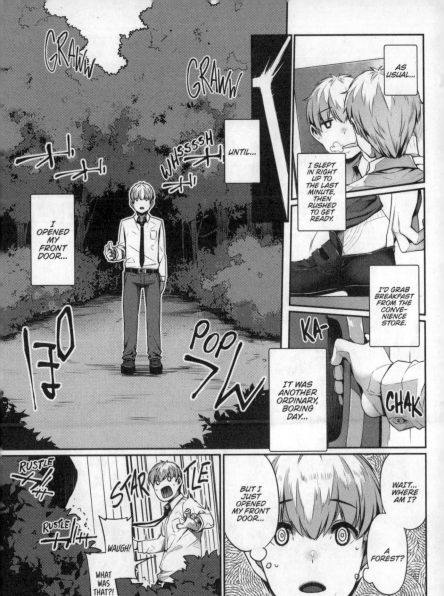

GRAWW

GRAWW

WHSSSSSH

UNTIL...

AS USUAL...

I SLEPT IN RIGHT UP TO THE LAST MINUTE, THEN RUSHED TO GET READY.

I OPENED MY FRONT DOOR...

I'D GRAB BREAKFAST FROM THE CONVENIENCE STORE.

POP

KA-

CHAK

IT WAS ANOTHER ORDINARY, BORING DAY...

RUSTLE

STARTLE

RUSTLE

WAUGH!

WHAT WAS THAT?!

BUT I JUST OPENED MY FRONT DOOR...

WAIT... WHERE AM I?

A FOREST?

AA-AH!
TAK
AA-AAA-HH!
TAK
RRRRRR
WHA-- ?!
RMMM
WHAT IN THE HELL IS THAT?!
HAAH!
WHAT THE HECK IS GOING--
THEY'RE NOT HUMAN, THAT'S FOR SURE!
HAAH!
HAAH!
WH
UMP
BGAH!
?!
FWOOOOOM

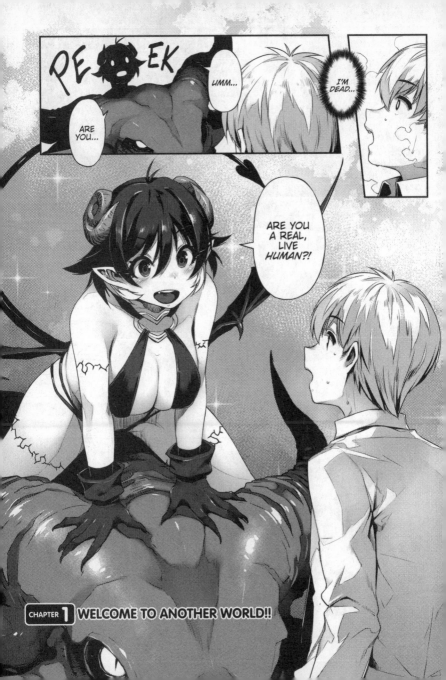

CHAPTER 1 WELCOME TO ANOTHER WORLD!!

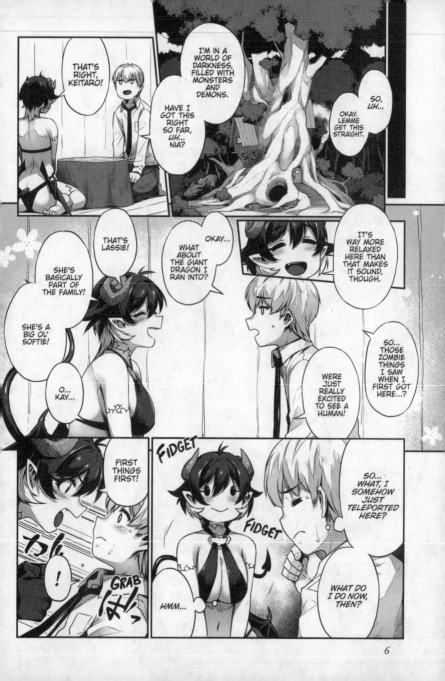

OKAY. LEMME GET THIS STRAIGHT.

HAVE I GOT THIS RIGHT SO FAR, UH... NIA?

THAT'S RIGHT, KEITARO!

I'M IN A WORLD OF DARKNESS, FILLED WITH MONSTERS AND DEMONS.

SO, UH...

OKAY... WHAT ABOUT THE GIANT DRAGON I RAN INTO?

THAT'S LASSIE!

SHE'S BASICALLY PART OF THE FAMILY!

SHE'S A BIG OL' SOFTIE!

O... KAY...

IT'S WAY MORE RELAXED HERE THAN THAT MAKES IT SOUND, THOUGH.

SO... THOSE ZOMBIE THINGS I SAW WHEN I FIRST GOT HERE...?

WERE JUST REALLY EXCITED TO SEE A HUMAN!

FIRST THINGS FIRST!

!

GRAB

FIDGET

FIDGET

HMM...

SO... WHAT, I SOMEHOW JUST TELEPORTED HERE?

WHAT DO I DO NOW, THEN?

6

I'M SO GLAD YOU'RE HERE!
BEAM
I'VE BEEN WAITING FOR SO LONG...
FOR YOU TO ARRIVE!
YOU'VE BEEN WAITING ...
FOR ME?
YEAH! I'LL GET STRAIGHT TO THE POINT!
KEITARO, I NEED YOU TO *MAKE BABIES* WITH ME!
BAM
HUH ?!
WHAT, LIKE, NOW ?!

UMM...
COULD YOU EXPLAIN WHY...?
OH! RIGHT!
I'M HALF DEVIL, AND HALF-DEVILS CAN ONLY REPRODUCE WITH HUMAN MEN!
I'VE BEEN WAITING SO MANY YEARS FOR A HUMAN TO APPEAR IN OUR WORLD!
I'VE ONLY MET ONE OTHER HUMAN BEFORE YOU, AND THAT'S MY DAD!
SO!
MAKE BABIES WITH ME!
I...
I GET IT, NOW...
Jiggle
BUT, UH...
I JUST GOT HERE, SO, UH...
OH, RIGHT...
PANIC
WAIT, I TOTALLY FORGOT!
JUMP

I GOTTA PUT TEA ON FOR MY GUEST!
YOU DON'T HAVE TO...
NO, I'LL BREW SOME RIGHT NOW. YOU WAIT RIGHT THERE! ♪
Glug
Glug Glug
FWOOSH
THIS TEA IS BREWED FROM MEDICINAL HERBS FOUND ONLY IN THIS WORLD!
THANKS!
OH...
IT'S WARM AND A LITTLE SWEET.
SLURP
...
IT'S ALSO...
KINDA MAKING ME HOT...?

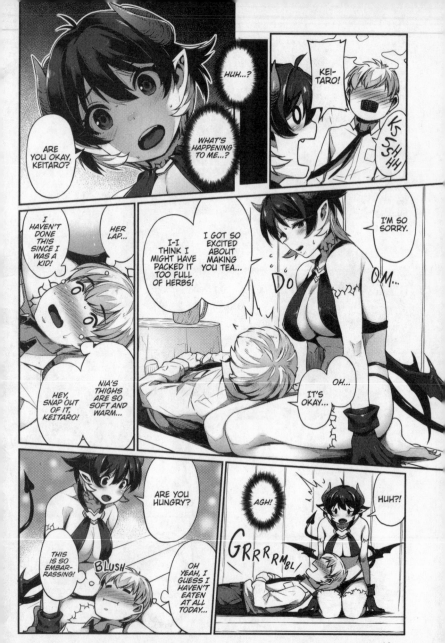

HUH...?

KEI-TARO!

ARE YOU OKAY, KEITARO?

WHAT'S HAPPENING TO ME...?

KSSSHH

I HAVEN'T DONE THIS SINCE I WAS A KID!

HER LAP...

I-I THINK I MIGHT HAVE PACKED IT TOO FULL OF HERBS!

I GOT SO EXCITED ABOUT MAKING YOU TEA...

I'M SO SORRY.

DO

O.M...

HEY, SNAP OUT OF IT, KEITARO!

NIA'S THIGHS ARE SO SOFT AND WARM...

OH...

IT'S OKAY...

ARE YOU HUNGRY?

AGH!

HUH?!

THIS IS SO EMBAR-RASSING!

BLUSH

OH YEAH, I GUESS I HAVEN'T EATEN AT ALL TODAY...

GRRRRMBL!

WAIT RIGHT THERE! I'LL GET YOU FOOD!
CAN I EVEN EAT STUFF FROM THIS WORLD...?
YEAH! JUST YOU LEAVE IT TO ME!
I'M A GREAT COOK!
WELL, I'M REALLY GOOD AT PEELING THE FRUITS AND VEGGIES OF THE FOREST!
PLANTS SHOULD BE SAFE, RIGHT?
IF I'D KNOWN YOU WERE COMING, I WOULD'VE COOKED YOU A NICE SLICE OF LIZARDMAN TAIL...
OH WELL!
BUT...
IT'LL BE COOKED WITH PLENTY OF LOVE!
JUST KIDDING!
SMOOCH
SLICE
SIZZLE
WHAT IS THAT?!
SLICE?

YIKES!
BLOOD!
GUSH
NIA?!
IT'S OKAY! I'LL JUST LICK IT TILL IT STOPS!
AHA HA HA!
BUT YOU'RE BLEEDING PRETTY BADLY...
OH, SHOOT, WAIT!
WHAT IS THIS, KEITARO?
SLAPPA
IT'S CALLED A BAND-AID.
UMM...
YOU PUT IT OVER CUTS!
I'M JUST GLAD I HAD ONE ON ME.
Blush
?
THANK YOU SO MUCH...
Squeeze
...!
BA-DUMP

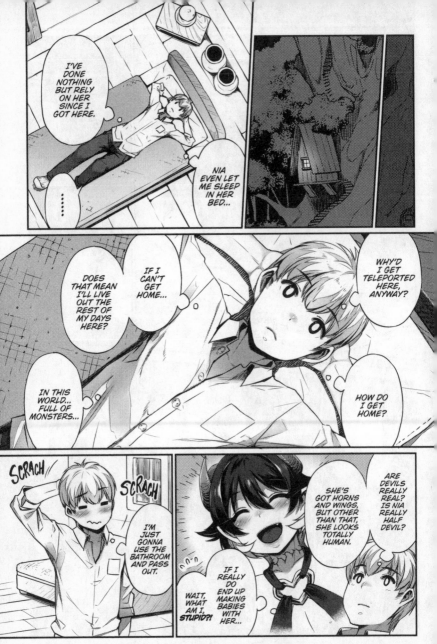

I'VE DONE NOTHING BUT RELY ON HER SINCE I GOT HERE.

......

NIA EVEN LET ME SLEEP IN HER BED...

DOES THAT MEAN I'LL LIVE OUT THE REST OF MY DAYS HERE?

IF I CAN'T GET HOME...

WHY'D I GET TELEPORTED HERE, ANYWAY?

IN THIS WORLD... FULL OF MONSTERS...

HOW DO I GET HOME?

SCRACH

SCRACH

I'M JUST GONNA USE THE BATHROOM AND PASS OUT.

SHE'S GOT HORNS AND WINGS, BUT OTHER THAN THAT, SHE LOOKS TOTALLY HUMAN.

ARE DEVILS REALLY REAL? IS NIA REALLY HALF DEVIL?

IF I REALLY DO END UP MAKING BABIES WITH HER...

WAIT, WHAT AM I, STUPID?!

...
PEEK
INFIL-
TRATION
INFIL-TRATION SUCCESS-FUL! ♪
RUSTLE
I GOT THIS LINGERIE AGES AGO, WAITING FOR THIS VERY MOMENT!
NOW I JUST GOTTA WAIT 'TIL HE GETS BACK IN BED!
I'M A GENIUS!
HEH HEH HEH!
RUSTLE
PHEW, I FEEL BETTER... HUH?
SOME-THING'S WRONG WITH MY BED...
WRIGGLE
WRIGGLE
OR RATHER, SOME-THING IN IT IS MOVING.
IS NIA TRYING TO PRANK ME?
GRAB
WHAT-EVER YOU ARE, I'M READY...!

WHAP
NIA'S FAST ASLEEP...
WAIT, WHAT THE HECK IS SHE WEARING?!
ZZZ
ZZZ...
IT'S TOTALLY SEE-THROUGH!
AND SHE'S NOT WEARING PANTIES!
WORRY
WORRY
AH, JEEZ... DON'T FREAK ME OUT LIKE THAT!
YOU'RE GONNA CATCH A COLD LIKE THIS.
TUG
...
Z Z Z
SWEET DREAMS, NIA...

TWEET
TWEET
TWEET
Sleepy
Sleepy
NOTHING'S GOING RIGHT AT ALL...!
BOW
BOW
DEPRESS
ION
I JUST WANTED TO SEDUCE HIM AND MAKE HIM MINE...
BUT INSTEAD I FREAKED HIM OUT AND HE HATES ME!
AT THIS RATE...
I'M NOT EVEN GONNA BE ABLE TO ASK ABOUT BABY-MAKING, LET ALONE ACTUALLY DO IT...
AFTER I WAITED SO LONG FOR A HUMAN...
I CAN'T JUST LET HIM GET AWAY!
I'VE GOTTA TRY HARDER!
I'LL SHOW KEITARO HOW GREAT I AM!
GRIP!

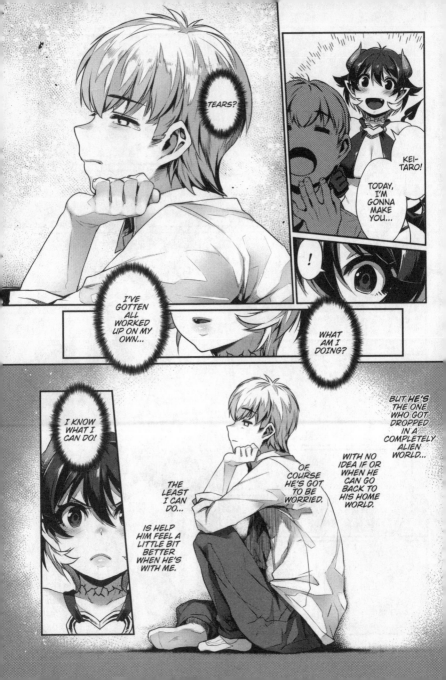

TEARS?

KEI-TARO!

TODAY, I'M GONNA MAKE YOU...

!

I'VE GOTTEN ALL WORKED UP ON MY OWN...

WHAT AM I DOING?

BUT HE'S THE ONE WHO GOT DROPPED IN A COMPLETELY ALIEN WORLD...

I KNOW WHAT I CAN DO!

WITH NO IDEA IF OR WHEN HE CAN GO BACK TO HIS HOME WORLD.

OF COURSE HE'S GOT TO BE WORRIED.

THE LEAST I CAN DO...

IS HELP HIM FEEL A LITTLE BIT BETTER WHEN HE'S WITH ME.

KEI-TARO!
YES, NIA?
THERE'S A REAL SPECIAL FRUIT I WANT YOU TO EAT, KEITARO!
I'M GONNA GO HARVEST SOME, SO JUST WAIT HERE 'TIL I COME BACK, OKAY?
OH, I'LL COME HELP!
NO, NO, YOU DON'T HAVE TO!
YOU'RE MY GUEST, AFTER ALL.
IT WON'T TAKE THAT LONG!
I'LL BE BACK IN A JIFFY!
WAVE
SEE YOU SOON!
OKAY, BE SAFE OUT THERE.
WAVE
...
......

SHE'S STILL NOT BACK!
IT'S GOTTEN DARK OUT, TOO...
SURE, SHE'S A HALF-DEVIL, BUT SHE'S A YOUNG WOMAN...
COULD SOMETHING HAVE HAPPENED TO HER?
MAYBE I SHOULD GO LOOK FOR HER.
BUT...
...
UGH, C'MON!
I CAN'T JUST SIT AROUND WORRYING!
HEY!
NIIIA!
CAN YOU HEAR ME?
RUSTLE
!
SWSH

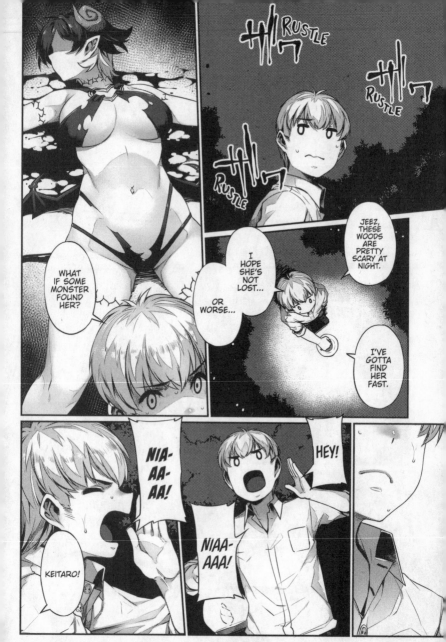

RUSTLE

RUSTLE

RUSTLE

JEEZ, THESE WOODS ARE PRETTY SCARY AT NIGHT.

WHAT IF SOME MONSTER FOUND HER?

I HOPE SHE'S NOT LOST...

OR WORSE...

I'VE GOTTA FIND HER FAST.

NIAA-AAA!

HEY!

NIAA-AAA!

KEITARO!

NIA! ARE YOU OKAY?!
I HURT MY ANKLE ON THE WAY BACK...
I WAS JUST GONNA REST UP A BIT AND SEE IF IT FELT BETTER.
OH...
SORRY TO WORRY YOU.

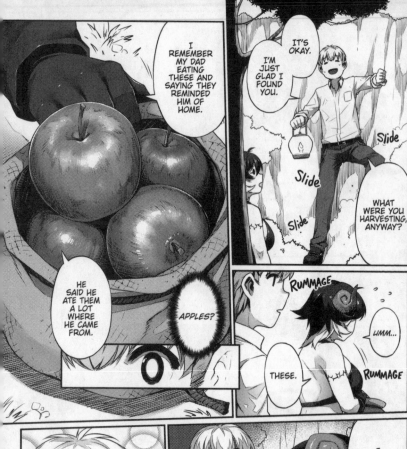

I REMEMBER MY DAD EATING THESE AND SAYING THEY REMINDED HIM OF HOME.

IT'S OKAY.

I'M JUST GLAD I FOUND YOU.

Slide

Slide

Slide

WHAT WERE YOU HARVESTING, ANYWAY?

HE SAID HE ATE THEM A LOT WHERE HE CAME FROM.

APPLES?

RUMMAGE

RUMMAGE

UMM...

THESE.

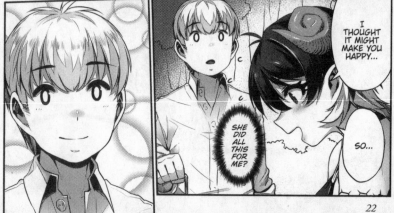

I THOUGHT IT MIGHT MAKE YOU HAPPY...

SHE DID ALL THIS FOR ME?

SO...

22

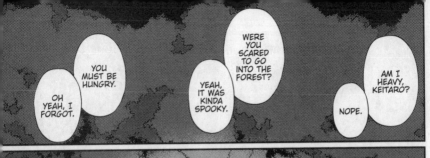

OH YEAH, I FORGOT.

YOU MUST BE HUNGRY.

YEAH, IT WAS KINDA SPOOKY.

WERE YOU SCARED TO GO INTO THE FOREST?

NOPE.

AM I HEAVY, KEITARO?

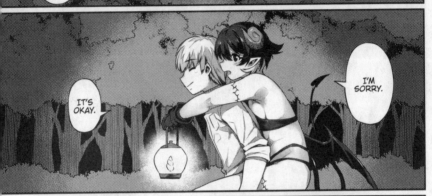

IT'S OKAY.

I'M SORRY.

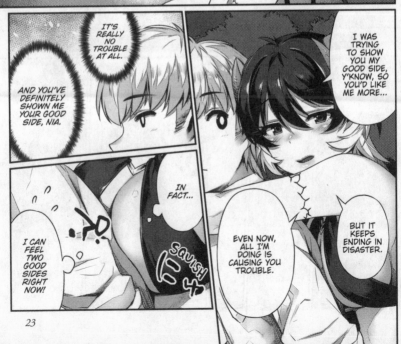

IT'S REALLY NO TROUBLE AT ALL.

AND YOU'VE DEFINITELY SHOWN ME YOUR GOOD SIDE, NIA.

I WAS TRYING TO SHOW YOU MY GOOD SIDE, Y'KNOW, SO YOU'D LIKE ME MORE...

IN FACT...

I CAN FEEL TWO GOOD SIDES RIGHT NOW!

SQUISH

EVEN NOW, ALL I'M DOING IS CAUSING YOU TROUBLE.

BUT IT KEEPS ENDING IN DISASTER.

23

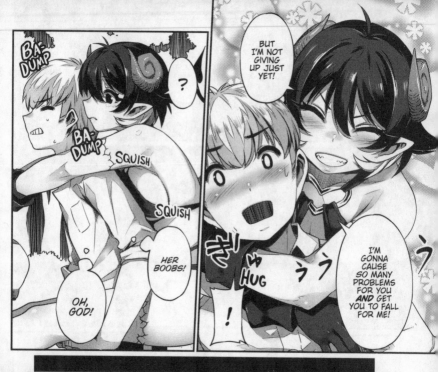

BA-DUMP

BA-DUMP

SQUISH

SQUISH

?

HER BOOBS!

OH, GOD!

BUT I'M NOT GIVING UP JUST YET!

HUG

I'M GONNA CAUSE SO MANY PROBLEMS FOR YOU *AND* GET YOU TO FALL FOR ME!

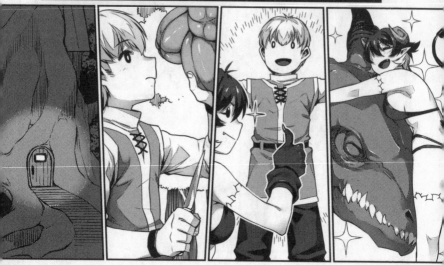

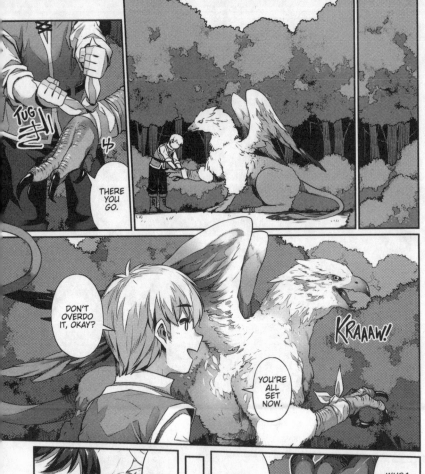

TUG

THERE YOU GO.

DON'T OVERDO IT, OKAY?

KRAAAW!

YOU'RE ALL SET NOW.

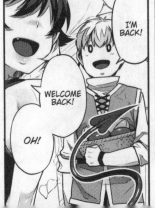

I'M BACK!

WELCOME BACK!

OH!

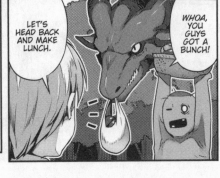

LET'S HEAD BACK AND MAKE LUNCH.

WHOA, YOU GUYS GOT A BUNCH!

WOULD YOU LIKE LUNCH?
A BATH?
OR MAYBE...
ME? ♡
LUNCH!
I'M STARVING!
AWWW!
YOU COULD AT LEAST GO ALONG WITH IT!
AHA HA HA!
DON'T LAUGH IT OFF! I'M BEING SERIOUS!

DEVILISH
DARLINGS
PORTAL
FANTASY

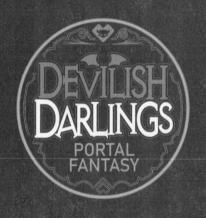

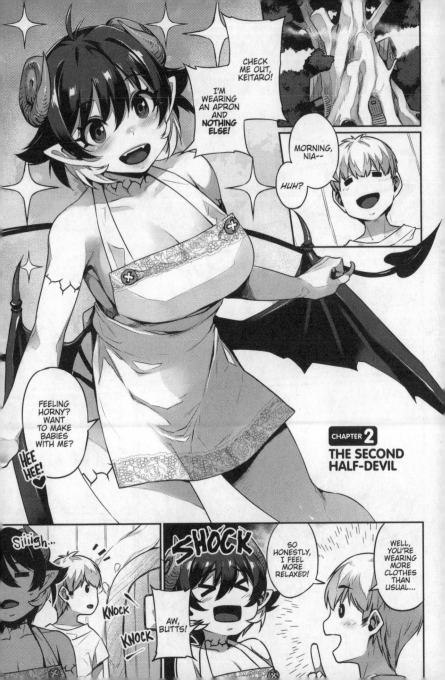

CHAPTER **2**
THE SECOND HALF-DEVIL

KER-CHAK
COMING!
HELLO!
I'M A WANDERING MERCHANT FROM THE FAIRY KINGDOM.
I HAVE ON MY PERSON MANY RARE GOODS!
BLOOD FRESHLY DRAWN FROM A RAINBOW LIZARD!
A SKULL RING THAT CAN NEVER BE TAKEN OFF!
SUCCUBUS MEDICINE THAT WILL CAUSE ANY BEING TO INSTANTLY FALL FOR YOU...
HUH?!
AND MORE...!
OH...
I DON'T SEE YOUR KIND AROUND MUCH.
LET ME INTRODUCE YOU!
THIS IS KEITARO! HE'S A **HUMAN** FROM ANOTHER WORLD!
H-HELLO.

WOW, A REAL LIFE HUMAN?
I'VE NEVER SEEN ONE IN THE FLESH BEFORE! ♪
I'VE HEARD TALES OF OTHER TRAVELERS GLIMPSING ANOTHER WORLD ON THEIR JOURNEYS, BUT WOW...
DOES THAT MEAN...
HUH?
WHO KNEW THE RUMORS WERE TRUE?! ♪
YOU GOTTA...
TELL US MORE ABOUT THOSE RUMORS!
EH...?
O- OH...

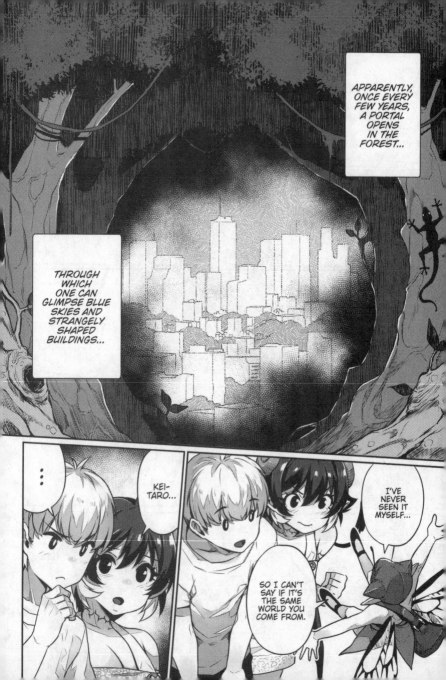

APPARENTLY, ONCE EVERY FEW YEARS, A PORTAL OPENS IN THE FOREST...

THROUGH WHICH ONE CAN GLIMPSE BLUE SKIES AND STRANGELY SHAPED BUILDINGS...

KEI-TARO...

I'VE NEVER SEEN IT MYSELF...

SO I CAN'T SAY IF IT'S THE SAME WORLD YOU COME FROM.

...
LET'S GO LOOK FOR IT, KEITARO!
HUH?!
YOU MIGHT BE ABLE TO MAKE IT BACK HOME!
SURE, BUT...
YOU'RE... OKAY WITH THAT, NIA?
OF COURSE!
MAKING BABIES IS IMPOR-TANT...
BUT GETTING YOU BACK TO YOUR HOME IS MORE IMPORTANT!
PLUS...
I CAN TRY TO GET YOU TO MAKE BABIES WITH ME ON THE TRIP!
MUA
HA HA!
N-NIA!
OH, RIGHT!
LET ME BUY SOME OF THAT SUCCUBUS MEDICINE...
...

THERE'S A LIZARDMAN OUTPOST NEARBY.
LET'S SUPPLY OURSELVES FOR THE TREK THERE!
WE SURE PICKED UP A LOT OF STUFF.
YOU OKAY CARRY-ING ALL THAT?
SURE, THIS IS NO SWEAT AT ALL!
THANKS AS ALWAYS!

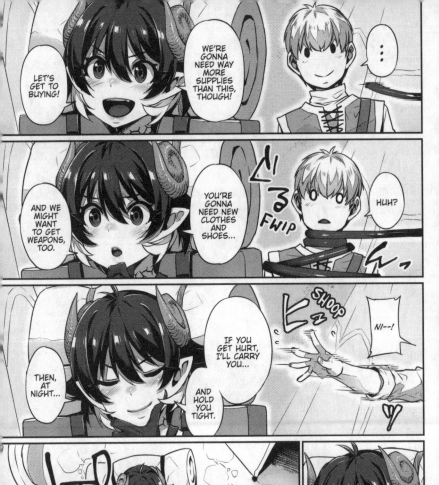

LET'S GET TO BUYING!

WE'RE GONNA NEED WAY MORE SUPPLIES THAN THIS, THOUGH!

...

AND WE MIGHT WANT TO GET WEAPONS, TOO.

YOU'RE GONNA NEED NEW CLOTHES AND SHOES...

FWIP

HUH?

THEN, AT NIGHT...

IF YOU GET HURT, I'LL CARRY YOU...

AND HOLD YOU TIGHT.

SHOOP

NI--!

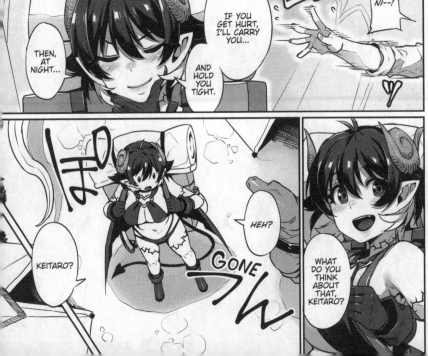

KEITARO?

HEH?

GONE

WHAT DO YOU THINK ABOUT THAT, KEITARO?

WELCOME TO MY ABODE. ♡
CLACK
FORGIVE MY MAN-HANDLING. ♡
I JUST NEVER SEE HUMANS WANDERING AROUND OUR WORLD. ♡
ぬ LOOM
SORRY TO RUSH INTO THINGS...
BAM!
IS SHE...
A HALF-DEVIL, TOO?!
BUT TO MAKE IT QUICK: I'M GONNA HAVE YOUR BABIES. ♡

JUST STAY STILL. THIS WON'T TAKE LONG.
JUST...
BE GOOD FOR ME...
SWEAT
OKAY...?
?!
H-HOLD UP A SEC!
I-I'M NOT READY!
AND, UH, YOU'RE REALLY SWEAT-ING--
GRAB
SHUT IT!
!

GASP
GASP
GASP
...
ドッ
THUMP
ドッ
THUMP
ドッ
THUMP
BADUMP
ドクンッ
BADUMP
ドクンッ
BADUMP
ドクーンッ
BADUMP
ドクンッ!!

KH!
SHOVE
I CAN'T.
I CAN'T DO IT...
SNIFFLE...
?!
TREMBLE
IS SHE...
TREMBLE
A... ARE YOU OKAY?

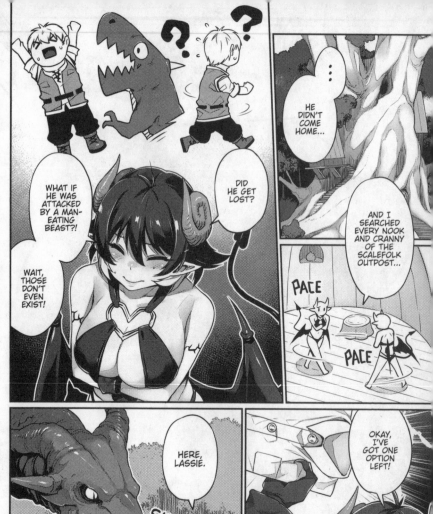

HE DIDN'T COME HOME...

WHAT IF HE WAS ATTACKED BY A MAN-EATING BEAST?!

DID HE GET LOST?

WAIT, THOSE DON'T EVEN EXIST!

AND I SEARCHED EVERY NOOK AND CRANNY OF THE SCALEFOLK OUTPOST...

PACE

PACE

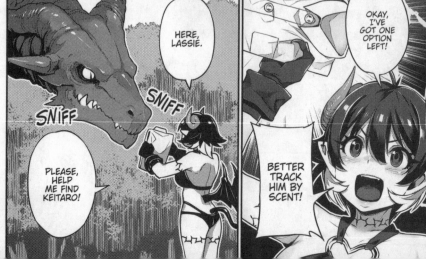

HERE, LASSIE.

SNIFF

SNIFF

PLEASE, HELP ME FIND KEITARO!

OKAY, I'VE GOT ONE OPTION LEFT!

BETTER TRACK HIM BY SCENT!

の
MOUNT
LET'S GO, LASSIE!
I'M COMING, KEITARO!
WHOOSH
NEVER FEEA-ARRRR!

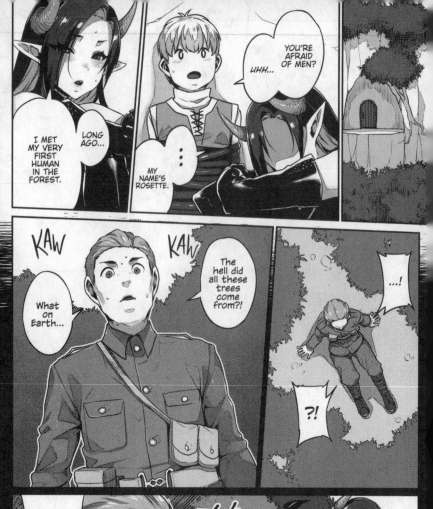

I MET MY VERY FIRST HUMAN IN THE FOREST.

LONG AGO...

UHH...

YOU'RE AFRAID OF MEN?

MY NAME'S ROSETTE.

KAW

KAW

What on Earth...

The hell did all these trees come from?!

....!

?!

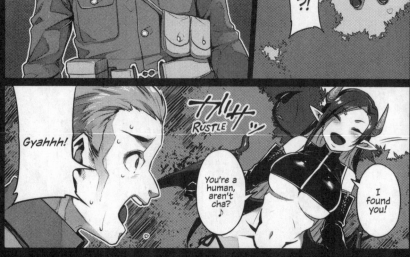

Gyahhh!

RUSTLE

You're a human, aren't cha? ♪

I found you!

Welcome!
I'm--
M-M-M-
Mon-ster!
クッ
SHOCKED
?!
AND I'VE BEEN AFRAID OF THEM...
EVER SINCE.
UMM...
THEN YOU DON'T HAVE TO, LIKE, *FORCE YOURSELF* TO HAVE ME.
...
I MEAN, YOU LOOK LIKE YOU'RE HAVING A HARD TIME.

BUT IF I LET YOU GO, I CAN'T HAVE BABIES.
NOT TO MEN-TION...
MY MOTHER ... IS SUPER SCARY.
GW-OOOO
SHE KEEPS ASKING ABOUT WHEN I'LL GIVE HER GRAND-CHILDREN...
HER MOM?!
HUH ?!
DON'T LAUGH AT ME!
I KNOW, A HALF-DEVIL WHO HATES MEN IS SUCH A JOKE!
THAT'S NOT WHY I'M LAUGH-ING...
YOU'RE JUST...
YOU'RE CUTE.
?!

C-CUTE...?
ARE YOU MAKING FUN OF ME?!
NO, NOOO!
I'M NOT MAKING FUN OF YOU AT ALL!
...
YOU'RE ACTING SUPER CUTE, IS ALL!
GRIN
GRIN
HMMM.
OKAY...

BOOM!!
DOOM
WAUGH!
NIA!
YEAH.
ARE YOU OKAY, KEI-TARO?!
I'M FINE...
DUNNO ABOUT ROS-ETTE...
キュ
CONK
OH?

MY GOODNESS...
ROSETTE, YOU CAN'T JUST STEAL ANOTHER WOMAN'S QUARRY!
YOU COULD HAVE HURT HIM, YOU KNOW?!
I'M SORRY!
WELL, KEITARO'S TOTALLY FINE...
SO I SUPPOSE I CAN LET YOU OFF THE HOOK. THIS ONCE.
OKAY, KEI-TARO...
WE GOT A LITTLE SIDE-TRACKED.
LET'S HEAD OUT!
OH!
...
WAIT!
?

PLEASE!
TAKE ME WITH YOU!
?!
I'VE CAUSED YOU BOTH SO MUCH TROUBLE...
AND I KNOW I'M IN NO POSITION TO ASK YOU FAVORS.
BUT, KEITARO...
I FEEL LIKE I'VE CHANGED A LITTLE, HAVING MET YOU.

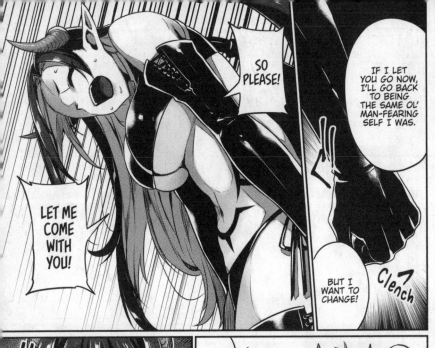

SO PLEASE!

IF I LET YOU GO NOW, I'LL GO BACK TO BEING THE SAME OL' MAN-FEARING SELF I WAS.

LET ME COME WITH YOU!

BUT I WANT TO CHANGE!

Clench

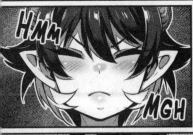

HMM

MGH

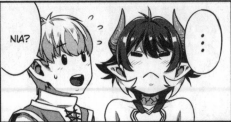

NIA?

...

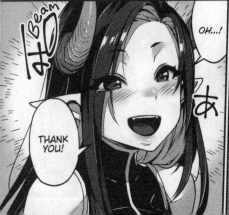

Beam

OH...!

THANK YOU!

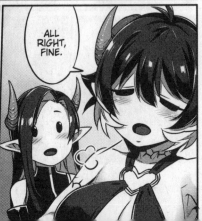

ALL RIGHT, FINE.

CRACKLE
BUT!
I GET TO MAKE BABIES WITH HIM *FIRST!*
CRACKLE
YOU'VE GOTTA GET USED TO EVEN **BEING** AROUND A GUY FIRST!
OH, I'M NOT SO SURE ABOUT THAT.
HAH?!
I MIGHT HAVE TO TAKE HIM FIRST. ♡
SURE, THAT'S TRUE.
HOW-EVER!
IF...
IT'S WITH KEI-TARO...
WHAT THE HELL ARE YOU IMPLYING?!
OH!
TRIP
WA-AH!
HUH?
GRAB

?!
RIP
URGH!
WHUMP
WHOA!

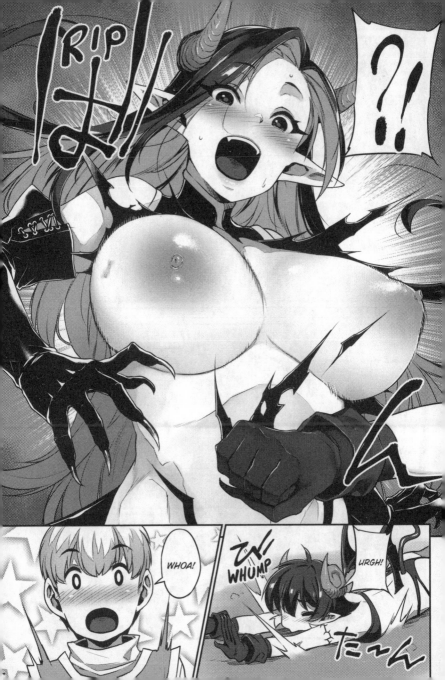

...
OWW.
I'M...
I- I'M NOT LOOKING! NOT AT ALL!
AH...
AAH...
AAAAAAAHH!
FWUMP
また
ROSETTE?!
HER FACE IS ALL RED!
WE'VE GOTTA GET SOMETHING TO COOL HER DOWN.
AND, UH, WE SHOULD COVER UP HER CHEST!
I DON'T HAVE ANYTHING THAT CAN DO THAT!

DEVILISH
DARLINGS
PORTAL
FANTASY

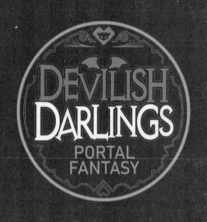

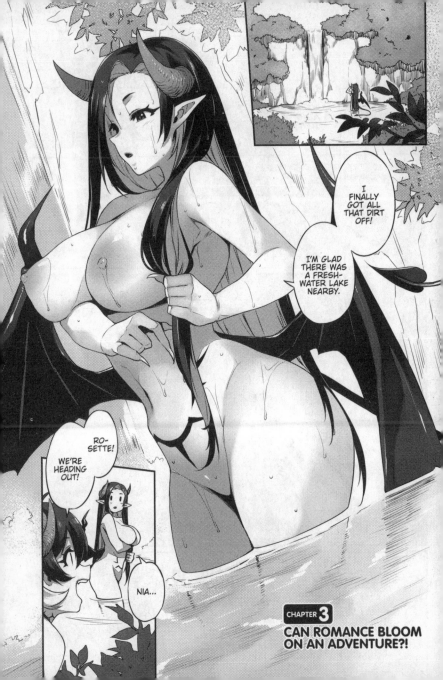

CHAPTER **3**
CAN ROMANCE BLOOM ON AN ADVENTURE?!

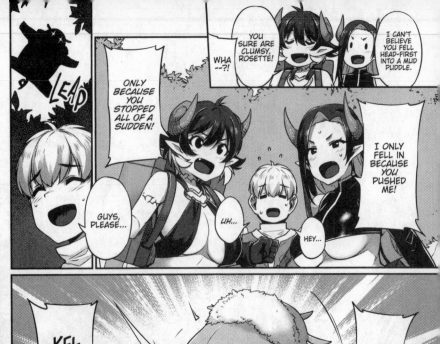

LEAP

YOU SURE ARE CLUMSY, ROSETTE!

WHA--?!

I CAN'T BELIEVE YOU FELL HEAD-FIRST INTO A MUD PUDDLE.

ONLY BECAUSE YOU STOPPED ALL OF A SUDDEN!

I ONLY FELL IN BECAUSE YOU PUSHED ME!

GUYS, PLEASE...

UH...

HEY...

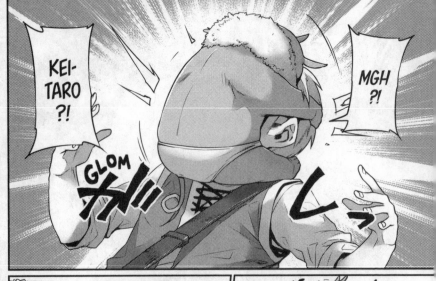

KEI-TARO?!

MGH ?!

GLOM

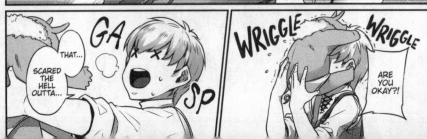

THAT... SCARED THE HELL OUTTA...

GA SP

WRIGGLE

WRIGGLE

ARE YOU OKAY?!

CHUB
WHAT ARE YOU?
IT LOOKS LIKE... AN ORC CHILD?
SNAP
CRACKLE
!
GRRRRRGH!
RAAAAARGH!
WHAP
WHA-AAA--?!

BOY, SORRY TO FREAK YOUSE OUT THERE!
THANKS FOR FINDIN' THE LI'L GUY FOR ME.
I SWEAR, THE SECOND MY EYES'RE OFF 'EM, THEY GO FLYIN' AWAY!
SO.
YOUSE GUYS LOOKIN' FOR THE PORTAL?
THAT'S RIGHT!
DO YOU KNOW ANY-THING ABOUT IT?
NOTHIN' TOO CONCRETE, BUT...
I'VE HEARD TELL IT'S REAL DEEP IN THE FOREST.
HOW DEEP?
RUMOR SEZ THAT IF YOUSE GO THAT DEEP IN THE FOREST, YOU AIN'T NEVER COMING OUT.
HUH?!
THAT SOUNDS PROMISING!

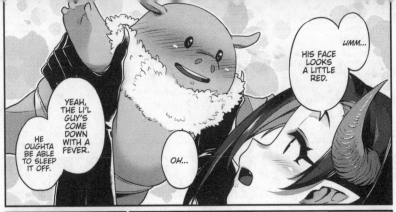

UMM... HIS FACE LOOKS A LITTLE RED.

YEAH, THE LI'L GUY'S COME DOWN WITH A FEVER.

HE OUGHTA BE ABLE TO SLEEP IT OFF.

OH...

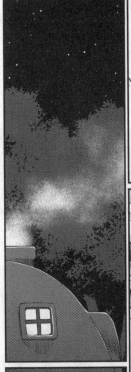

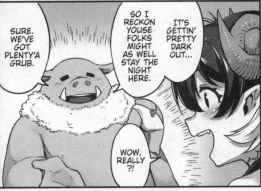

IT'S GETTIN' PRETTY DARK OUT...

SO I RECKON YOUSE FOLKS MIGHT AS WELL STAY THE NIGHT HERE.

SURE. WE'VE GOT PLENTY'A GRUB.

WOW, REALLY?!

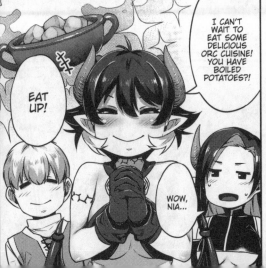

I CAN'T WAIT TO EAT SOME DELICIOUS ORC CUISINE! YOU HAVE BOILED POTATOES?!

EAT UP!

WOW, NIA...

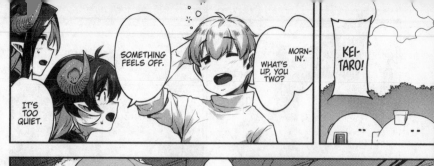

IT'S TOO QUIET.

SOMETHING FEELS OFF.

WHAT'S UP, YOU TWO?

MORN-IN'.

KEI-TARO!

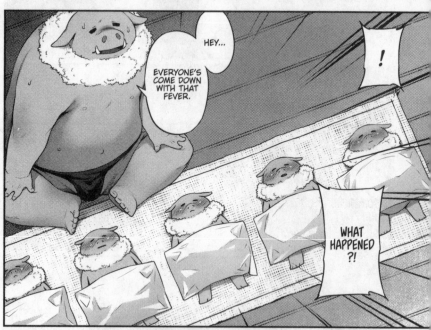

HEY...

EVERYONE'S COME DOWN WITH THAT FEVER.

!

WHAT HAPPENED?!

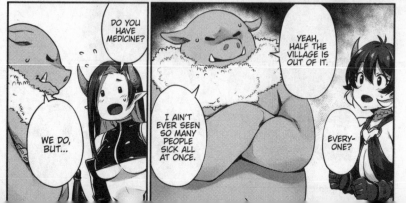

DO YOU HAVE MEDICINE?

WE DO, BUT...

YEAH, HALF THE VILLAGE IS OUT OF IT.

I AIN'T EVER SEEN SO MANY PEOPLE SICK ALL AT ONCE.

EVERY-ONE?

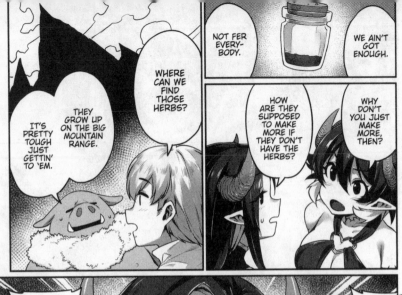

WHERE CAN WE FIND THOSE HERBS?

THEY GROW UP ON THE BIG MOUNTAIN RANGE.

IT'S PRETTY TOUGH JUST GETTIN' TO 'EM.

NOT FER EVERY-BODY.

WE AIN'T GOT ENOUGH.

HOW ARE THEY SUPPOSED TO MAKE MORE IF THEY DON'T HAVE THE HERBS?

WHY DON'T YOU JUST MAKE MORE, THEN?

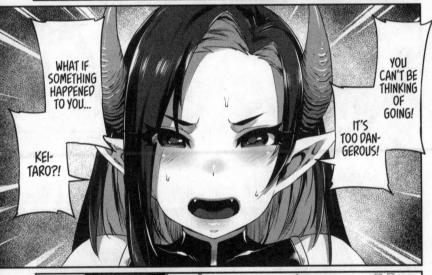

WHAT IF SOMETHING HAPPENED TO YOU...

KEI-TARO?!

YOU CAN'T BE THINKING OF GOING!

IT'S TOO DAN-GEROUS!

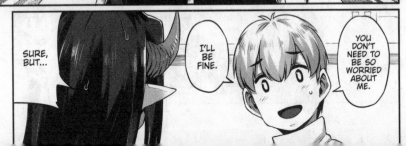

SURE, BUT...

I'LL BE FINE.

YOU DON'T NEED TO BE SO WORRIED ABOUT ME.

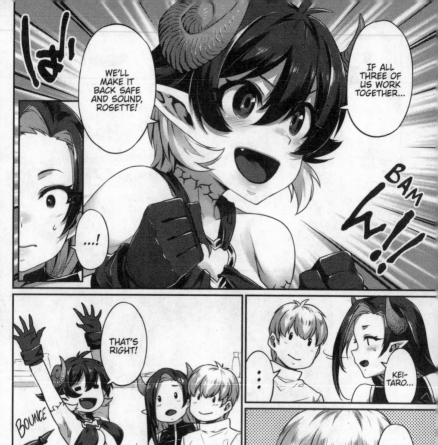

WE'LL MAKE IT BACK SAFE AND SOUND, ROSETTE!

IF ALL THREE OF US WORK TOGETHER...

....

BAM!!

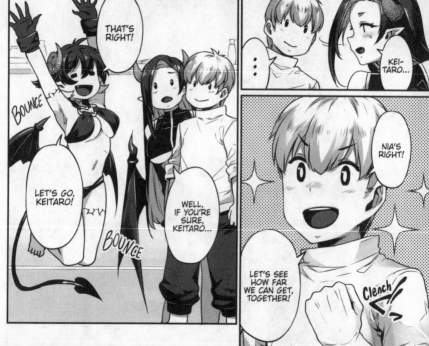

THAT'S RIGHT!

LET'S GO, KEITARO!

WELL, IF YOU'RE SURE, KEITARO...

BOUNCE

BOUNCE

...

KEI-TARO...

NIA'S RIGHT!

LET'S SEE HOW FAR WE CAN GET, TOGETHER!

Clench!

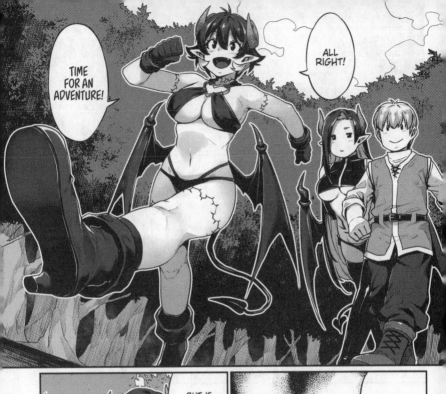

TIME FOR AN ADVENTURE!

ALL RIGHT!

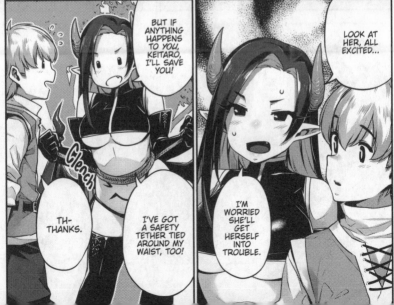

BUT IF ANYTHING HAPPENS TO *YOU*, KEITARO, I'LL SAVE YOU!

LOOK AT HER, ALL EXCITED...

Glench

TH- THANKS.

I'VE GOT A SAFETY TETHER TIED AROUND MY WAIST, TOO!

I'M WORRIED SHE'LL GET HERSELF INTO TROUBLE.

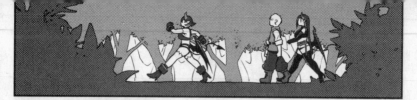

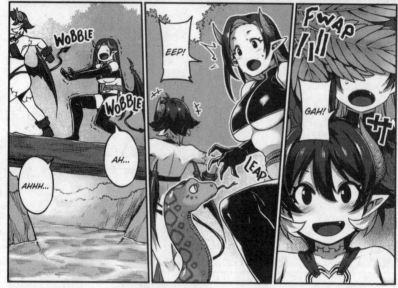

WOBBLE

WOBBLE

AHHH...

AH...

EEP!

FWAP

GAH!

LEAP

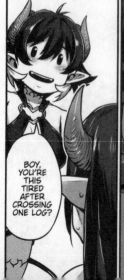

BOY, YOU'RE THIS TIRED AFTER CROSSING ONE LOG?

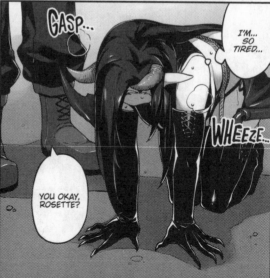

GASP...

I'M... SO TIRED...

WHEEZE...

YOU OKAY, ROSETTE?

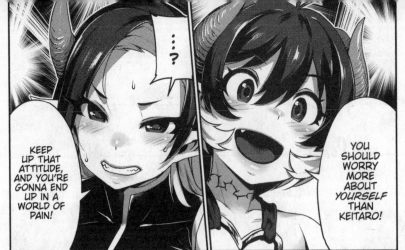

KEEP UP THAT ATTITUDE, AND YOU'RE GONNA END UP IN A WORLD OF PAIN!

...?

YOU SHOULD WORRY MORE ABOUT *YOURSELF* THAN KEITARO!

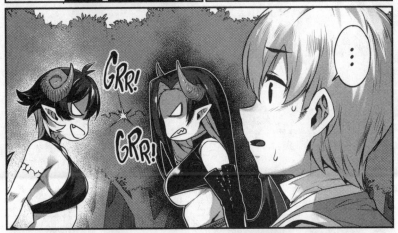

GRR!

GRR!

...

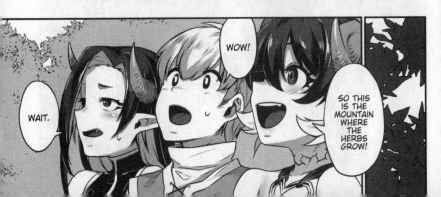

WAIT.

WOW!

SO THIS IS THE MOUNTAIN WHERE THE HERBS GROW!

THIS LOOKS...
LOOoooOM
WAY MORE INTENSE THAN I THOUGHT!
I DON'T KNOW IF WE CAN MAKE IT ALL THE WAY UP...
MAYBE WE SHOULD CALL FOR HELP, OR GET MORE EQUIPMENT?
RO-SETTE!
WE DON'T HAVE TIME FOR THAT!

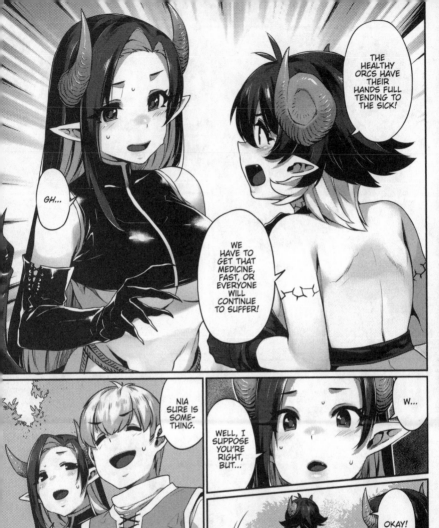

THE HEALTHY ORCS HAVE THEIR HANDS FULL TENDING TO THE SICK!

GH...

WE HAVE TO GET THAT MEDICINE, FAST, OR EVERYONE WILL CONTINUE TO SUFFER!

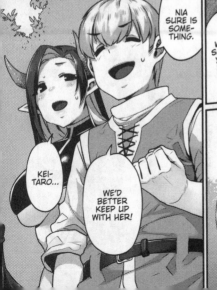

NIA SURE IS SOMETHING.

WELL, I SUPPOSE YOU'RE RIGHT, BUT...

W....

KEI-TARO...

WE'D BETTER KEEP UP WITH HER!

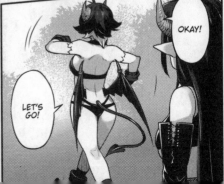

OKAY!

LET'S GO!

HAAH!
HAAH!
KEITARO!
DON
ARE YOU OKAY?
THANKS, NIA.
THIS IS PRETTY ROUGH.
WATCH WHERE YOU'RE WALKING!
IF YOU FALL DOWN LIKE YOU *ALWAYS* DO, YOU'RE GONNA END UP TRIPPING KEITARO!
DON'T WORRY!
I'LL DODGE KEITARO AND SMACK INTO YOU INSTEAD, ROSETTE!

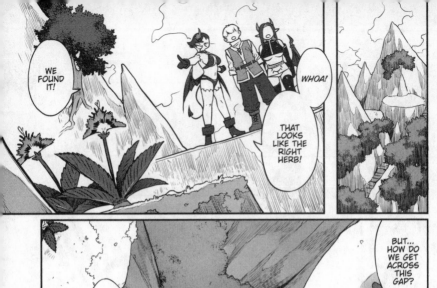

WE FOUND IT!

WHOA!

THAT LOOKS LIKE THE RIGHT HERB!

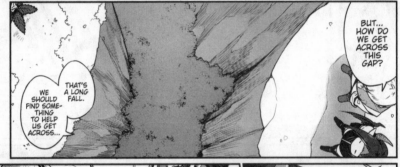

BUT... HOW DO WE GET ACROSS THIS GAP?

WE SHOULD FIND SOMETHING TO HELP US GET ACROSS...

THAT'S A LONG FALL.

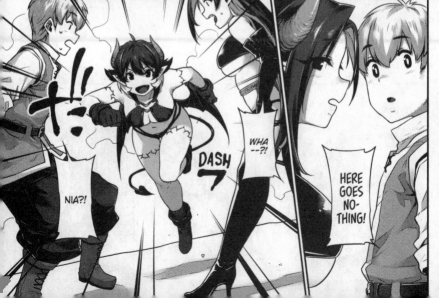

NIA?!

DASH

WHA --?!

HERE GOES NOTHING!

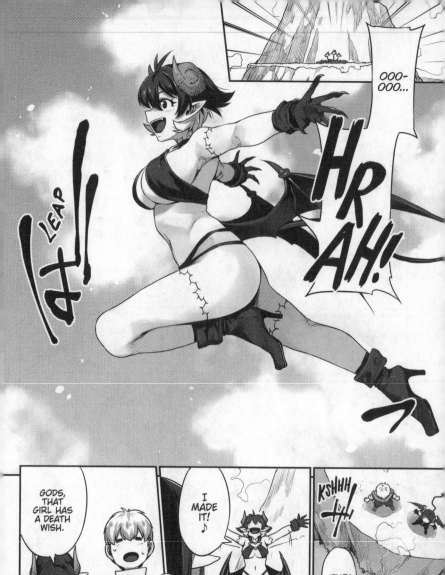

OOO-OOO...

LEAP

HR AH!

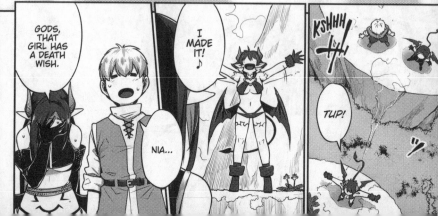

GODS, THAT GIRL HAS A DEATH WISH.

I MADE IT! ♪

NIA...

KSHHH

TUP!

BUT THIS MEANS WE CAN MAKE THE MEDICINE!
RIGHT.
WHOA!
ギッ
CRUMBLE
BE CAREFUL, NIA!
YEAH, YEAH, I'LL BE BACK IN A JIFFY!
LEAP
HUH?!
NOOO!
NIA!

CREEE-
EEEAK
LIKE I SAID, DEATH WISH...
...

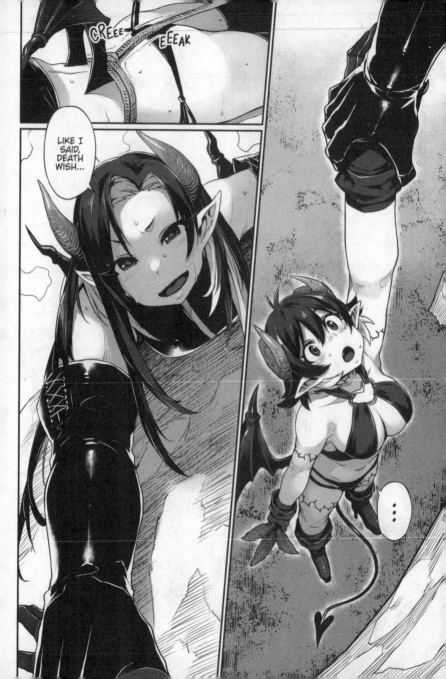

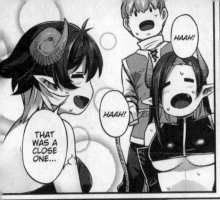

HAAH!
HAAH!
THAT WAS A CLOSE ONE...
IS THAT ALL YOU'VE GOT TO SAY TO ME?!
YOU WERE THIS CLOSE TO DYING!
IF I HADN'T CAUGHT YOU, YOU'D BE SMEARED ACROSS THE BOTTOM OF THAT GORGE!
URGH...
I'M SORRY.
SULK
SHEESH.
WE WERE WORRIED SICK.

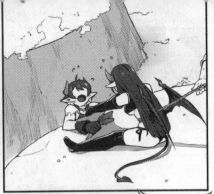

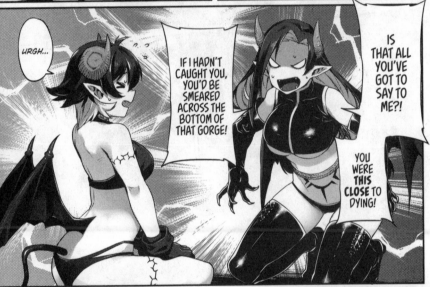

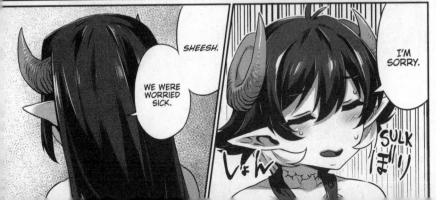

SO PLEASE...
BE A LITTLE MORE CAREFUL.
OKAY?
OOO-KAY.
THANKS...
ROSETTE.
...
ALL RIGHT, LET'S HEAD BACK TO THE VILLAGE!
YEAH!

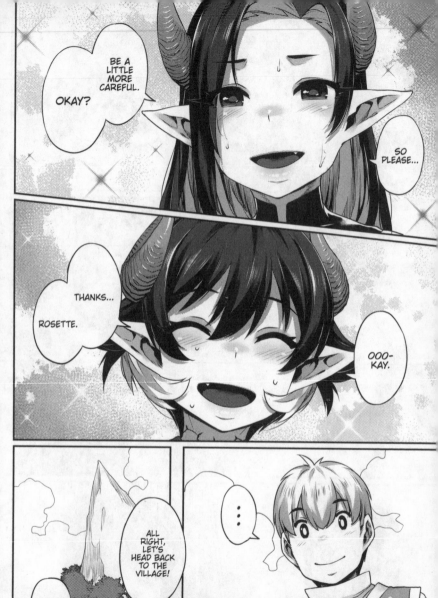

WE'RE FEELIN' MUCH BETTER, AND IT'S ALL THANKS TO YOUSE GUYS.
I DUNNO HOW TO REPAY YOUSE.
YOU DON'T HAVE TO! WE GOT TO SAMPLE ALL THAT YUMMY FOOD.
YOU NEED TO LEARN SOME RESTRAINT, NIA.
I HOPE YOUSE FIND WHAT YOUSE LOOKIN' FOR!
THANKS!
SAFE TRAVELS, FRIENDS!
WE'LL BE BACK!

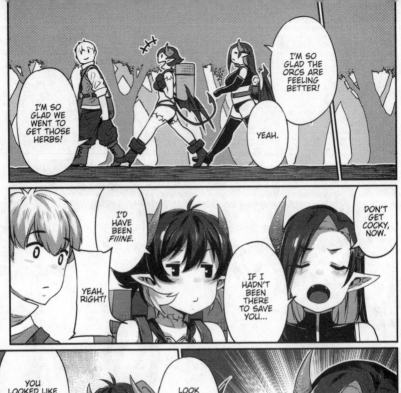

I'M SO GLAD WE WENT TO GET THOSE HERBS!

I'M SO GLAD THE ORCS ARE FEELING BETTER!

YEAH.

I'D HAVE BEEN FIIINE.

YEAH, RIGHT!

DON'T GET COCKY, NOW.

IF I HADN'T BEEN TO SAVE YOU...

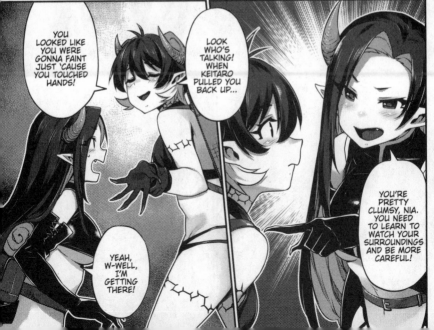

YOU LOOKED LIKE YOU WERE GONNA FAINT JUST 'CAUSE YOU TOUCHED HANDS!

LOOK WHO'S TALKING! WHEN KEITARO PULLED YOU BACK UP...

YEAH, W-WELL, I'M GETTING THERE!

YOU'RE PRETTY CLUMSY, NIA. YOU NEED TO LEARN TO WATCH YOUR SURROUNDINGS AND BE MORE CAREFUL!

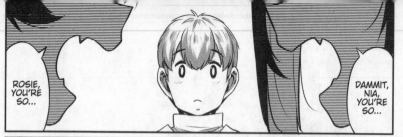

ROSIE, YOU'RE SO...

DAMMIT, NIA, YOU'RE SO...

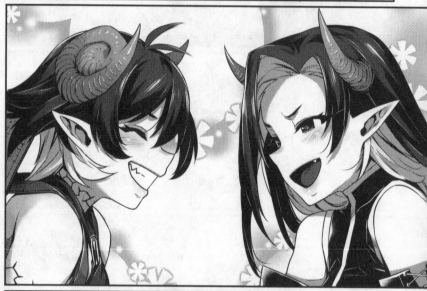

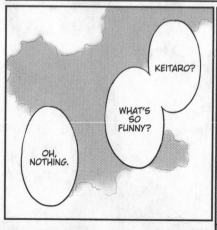

KEITARO?

WHAT'S SO FUNNY?

OH, NOTHING.

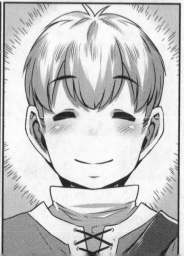

DEVILISH DARLINGS
PORTAL FANTASY

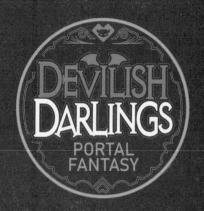

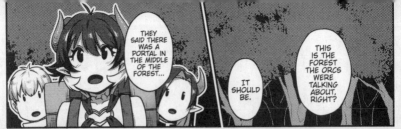

THEY SAID THERE WAS A PORTAL IN THE MIDDLE OF THE FOREST...

IT SHOULD BE.

THIS IS THE FOREST THE ORCS WERE TALKING ABOUT, RIGHT?

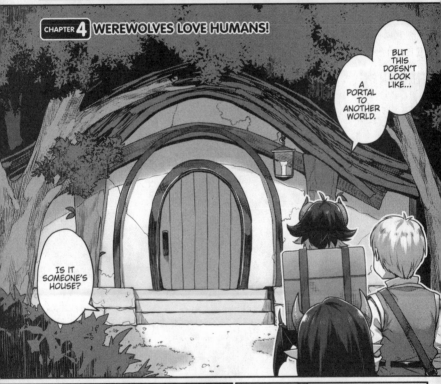

CHAPTER 4 WEREWOLVES LOVE HUMANS!

BUT THIS DOESN'T LOOK LIKE...

A PORTAL TO ANOTHER WORLD.

IS IT SOMEONE'S HOUSE?

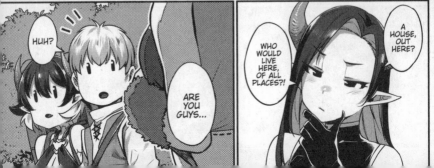

HUH?

ARE YOU GUYS...

WHO WOULD LIVE HERE, OF ALL PLACES?!

A HOUSE, OUT HERE?

GUESTS ?!
Beam
はぁあっ
WOW!
WELCOME TO MY HUMBLE HOME!
WAG
WAG
?!

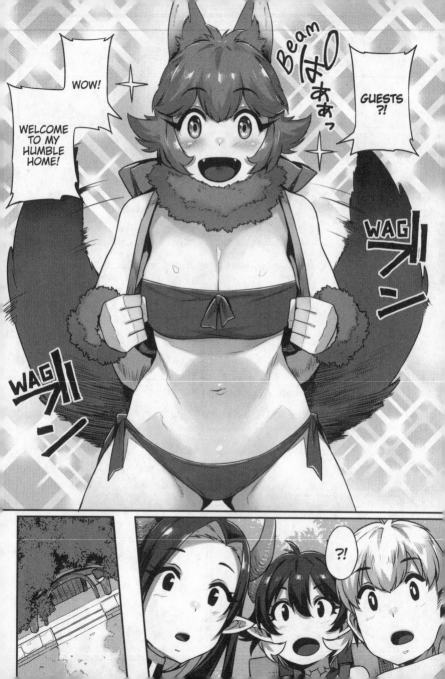

I'M MONAY! I'M A WEREWOLF!
I LIVE HERE BY MYSELF!
IT'S GREAT TO MEET YOU!
I CAN'T BELIEVE YOU CAME ALL THIS WAY JUST TO SEE ME...
SPARKLE
SPARKLE
I'M TOUCHED!
OH, UH...
WE DIDN'T COME HERE TO SEE YOU, ACTUALLY.
DEVA-STATED...
OH... OKAY.
YOU SEE...

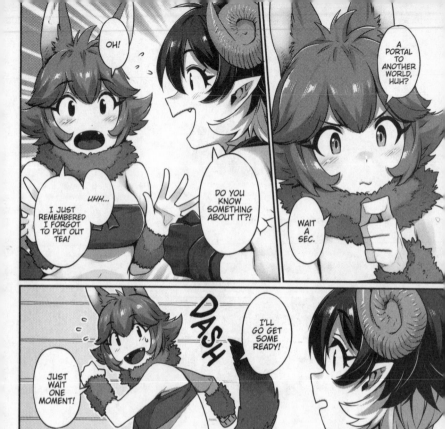

OH!

A PORTAL TO ANOTHER WORLD, HUH?

UHH...

I JUST REMEMBERED I FORGOT TO PUT OUT TEA!

DO YOU KNOW SOMETHING ABOUT IT?!

WAIT A SEC.

DASH

I'LL GO GET SOME READY!

JUST WAIT ONE MOMENT!

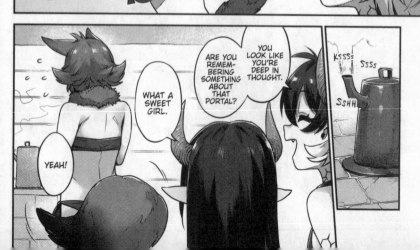

WHAT A SWEET GIRL.

ARE YOU REMEMBERING SOMETHING ABOUT THAT PORTAL?

YOU LOOK LIKE YOU'RE DEEP IN THOUGHT.

KSSSS SSSS

SSHH

YEAH!

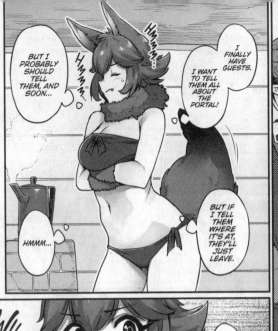

BUT I PROBABLY SHOULD TELL THEM, AND SOON...

HMMM...

HMMM...

HMMM...

I FINALLY HAVE GUESTS.

I WANT TO TELL THEM ALL ABOUT THE PORTAL!

HMMM...

BUT IF I TELL THEM WHERE IT'S AT, THEY'LL JUST LEAVE.

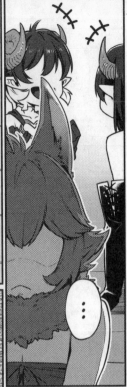

...

WHIP

STILL!

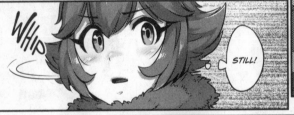

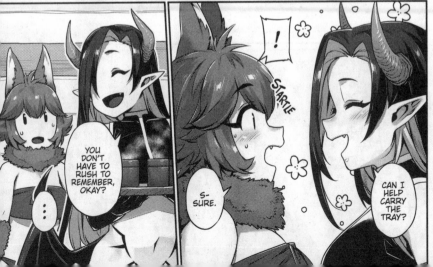

!

STARTLE

YOU DON'T HAVE TO RUSH TO REMEMBER, OKAY?

S-SURE.

...

CAN I HELP CARRY THE TRAY?

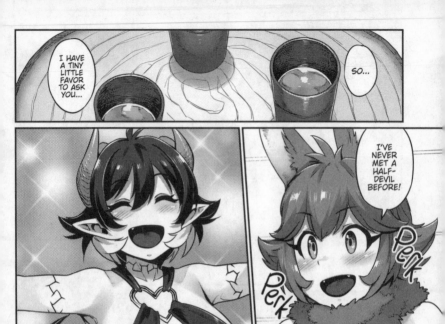

SO...

I HAVE A TINY LITTLE FAVOR TO ASK YOU...

I'VE NEVER MET A HALF-DEVIL BEFORE!

Perk *Perk*

SURE, COME HERE!

COULD I TOUCH YOUR WINGS?!

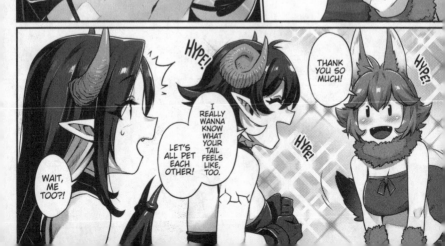

HYPE!

I REALLY WANNA KNOW WHAT YOUR TAIL FEELS LIKE, TOO.

LET'S ALL PET EACH OTHER!

THANK YOU SO MUCH!

HYPE!

WAIT, ME TOO?!

HYPE!

EXCUSE ME...
WOULD IT BE OKAY IF I TOUCH *YOUR* BODY A LITTLE, TOO?
OF COURSE!

WOW!
NO WINGS OR TAIL!
NO HORNS OR FANGS!
SQUISH
SQUISH
...
HRRM! LET'S SEE HOW YOU TASTE...!
WHOA!
ペロッ
Looolick
HUH ?!

PULL
PULL
OKAY, THAT'S ENOUGH!
GET OFF HIM!
JUST A LITTLE MORE!
PULL
YA
NK
OH.
WAAAAAH!
TUMBLE
TUMBLE
?!

AGH!
WHAM
ARE YOU OKAY?!
NIA!
MO-NAY!
BA-DUMP
!
CHIRP
CHIRP
CHIRP
OWIE, OW, OW...
OKAY, MAYBE I GOT A LITTLE CARRIED AWAY.
BWUH?

YOU BROKE DOWN THE DOOR AND TUMBLED OUTSIDE?

SHEESH, KEEP IT TOGETHER.

YOU SCARED ME THERE!

MAN, I COULDN'T STOP TUMBLING!

I'M ALL DIZZY!

Seethe

Seethe

MO...

NAY?

KRICK

KRICK

SHINK

SHINK

...

MONAY, YOU OKAY?

NIA!

GET AWAY FROM HER!

!

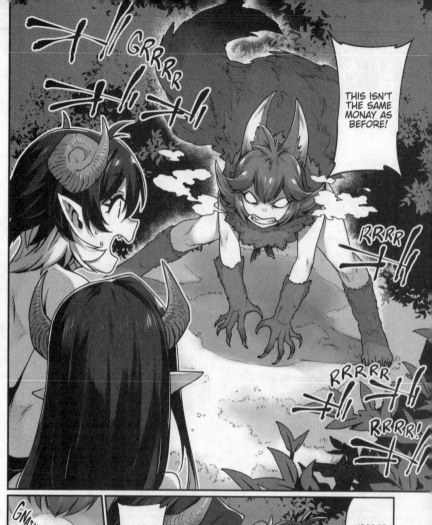

GRRRR

RRRR

RRRRR

RRRR!

THIS ISN'T THE SAME MONAY AS BEFORE!

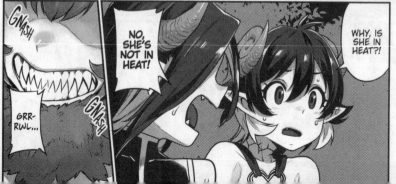

GNASH

GNASH

GRR-RWL...

NO, SHE'S NOT IN HEAT!

WHY, IS SHE IN HEAT?!

WATCH OUT!
SNARL!
SHE'S GONE TOTALLY MAD!
KSSS
SHHH
NO-THING LEFT TO DO...
BUT STOP HER BY **FORCE!**
GRAWR!

HNNGH!
WRESTLE
GRAGH!
SHE'S SO STRONG!
STRAIN
I CAN'T BEAT HER!
THIS IS NO GOOD!
HOLD... HOLD ON!
SHING

LICK
NO!
LICK
DON'T LICK ME THERE!
AH!
LICK
LICK
...!
LICK
NO!
AAAAAH!
LICK
Haaah
Haaah
ROSETTE!
Slobber
GRRR!
TURN
SWIPE
AHH!
GRAB

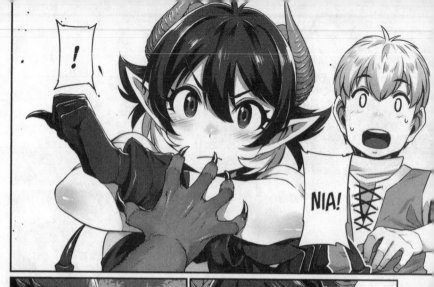

NIA!

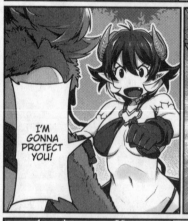

I'M GONNA PROTECT YOU!

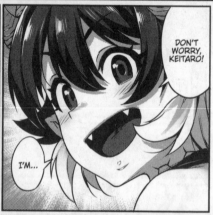

DON'T WORRY, KEITARO!

I'M...

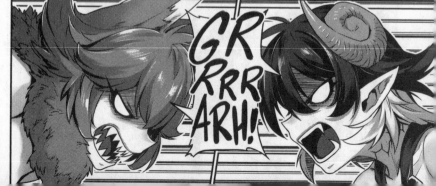

GR RRR ARH!

AGH!
TRIP
…
SLIIIIDE
NIA!
?!
GRAB
WAIT!
MON--
…!
WHUMP

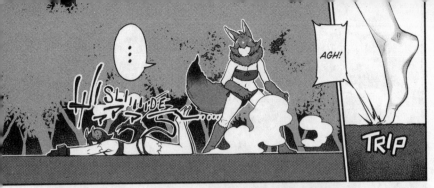

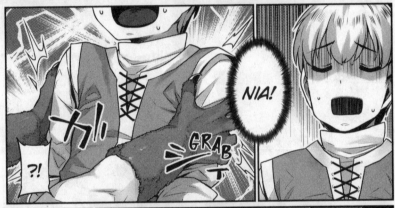

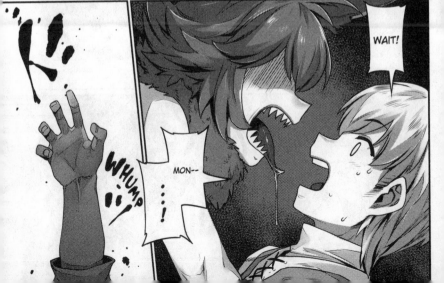

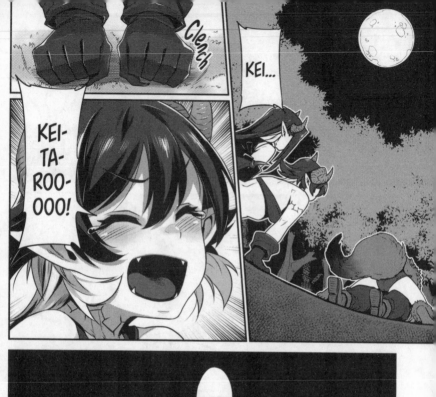

Clench

KEI...

KEI-TA-ROO-OOO!

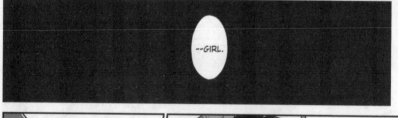

--GIRL.

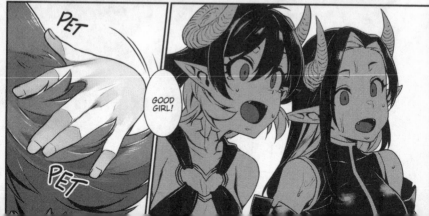

PET

GOOD GIRL!

PET

PET なで
HAAH!
HAAH!
GOOD GIRL!
PET なで
HAAH!
SUCH A GOOD GIRL!
なで PET
PET なで

WHO'S A GOOD GIRL? YOU ARE!
GOOD GIRL...
...
I AM SO SORRY FOR WHAT HAPPENED LAST NIGHT!
PLEASE FORGIVE ME!
YOU REALLY SCARED US OUT THERE!
I'M MORTI-FIED!
FORGIVE MEEE!

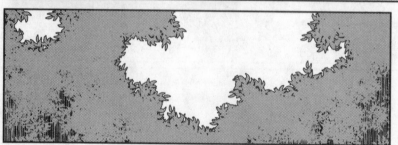

WERE-WOLVES GET REALLY WORKED UP WHEN THEY SEE THE FULL MOON.
THEY JUST START LICKING AND HUGGING ANYONE AROUND THEM!
YOU SURE GOT SLOBBERED ALL OVER, ROSIE.
YOU DON'T HAVE TO BRING IT UP, SHEESH!
I MOVED OUT HERE TO THE FOREST...
SO I WOULDN'T BOTHER ANYONE IF OR WHEN I WENT MOON-CRAZY.
DROOP...
I WAS SO EXCITED TO FINALLY HAVE VISITORS...
I TOTALLY FORGOT YESTERDAY WAS THE FULL MOON.
BOY, THOUGH, I HAD NO IDEA...
THAT KEITARO WAS SO GOOD WITH WERE-WOLVES!
I WAS SURPRISED, TOO!
Beam
I HAD A DOG BACK HOME, SO I'M GOOD AT PETTING DOGS.
BLUSH

GRAB
SIIIIGH
KEI-TARO!
I HAD NO IDEA GETTING PETTED BY A HUMAN COULD FEEL SO GOOD!
I BET I COULD GET TOTALLY ADDICTED TO IT! ♡
HUH?
SPARKLE
HUH?!
IF YOU DON'T MIND...
SPARKLE
WOULD YOU PET ME AGAIN TONIGHT?
GRIP

A GRUMP
GRUMP
CAN'T TAKE MY EYE OFF YOU FOR A SECOND!
THAT'S A LITTLE TOO CLOSE!
OKAY!
WAUGH!
UMM...
COME BY AGAIN ANYTIME, IF YOU WANT!
OF COURSE!
YOU HAVE TO GO ALREADY? BUT WE JUST MET!
I WISH YOU COULD STAY...
DISAP-POINTED

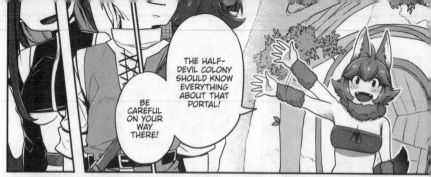

THE HALF-DEVIL COLONY SHOULD KNOW EVERYTHING ABOUT THAT PORTAL!

BE CAREFUL ON YOUR WAY THERE!

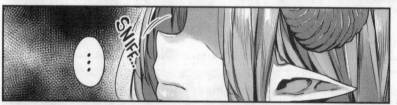

SNIFF...

...

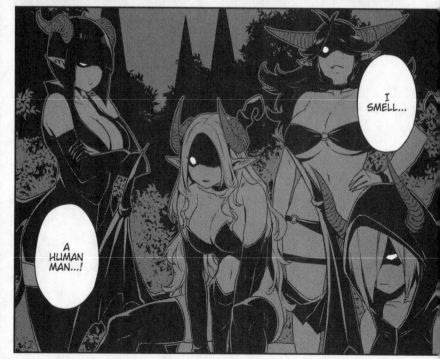

I SMELL...

A HUMAN MAN...!

DEVILISH
DARLINGS
PORTAL
FANTASY

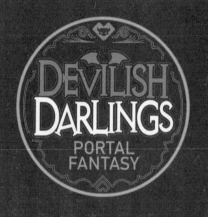

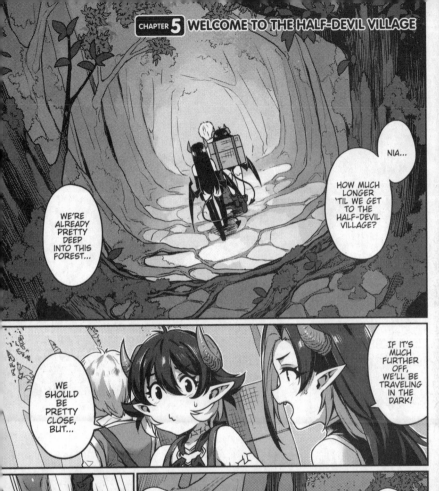

NIA...

HOW MUCH LONGER 'TIL WE GET TO THE HALF-DEVIL VILLAGE?

WE'RE ALREADY PRETTY DEEP INTO THIS FOREST...

IF IT'S MUCH FURTHER OFF, WE'LL BE TRAVELING IN THE DARK!

WE SHOULD BE PRETTY CLOSE, BUT...

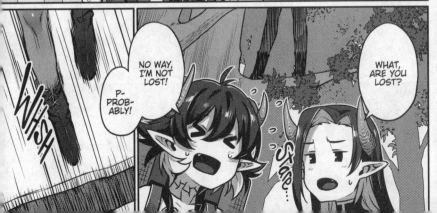

WHAT, ARE YOU LOST?

NO WAY, I'M NOT LOST!

P-PROB-ABLY!

WHSH

Stare...

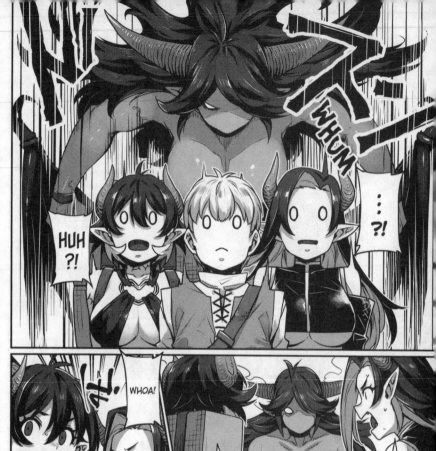

HUH ?!

... ?!

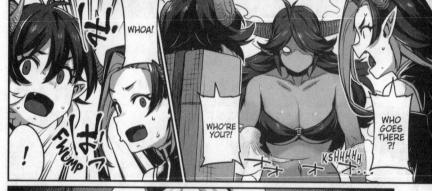

WHOA!

WHO'RE YOU?!

WHO GOES THERE ?!

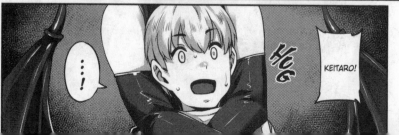

...

KEITARO!

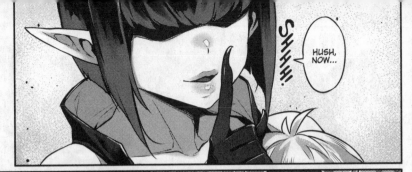

SHHH!

HUSH, NOW...

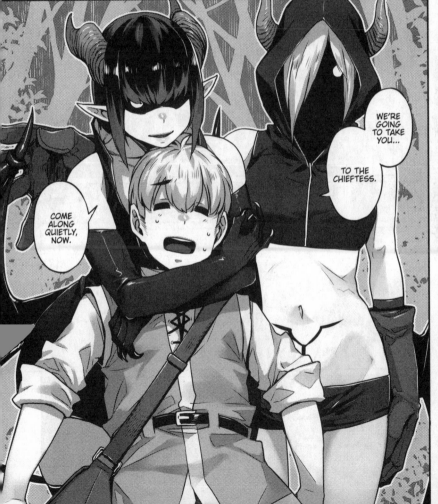

WE'RE GOING TO TAKE YOU...

TO THE CHIEFTESS.

COME ALONG QUIETLY, NOW.

WELCOME, TRAVELERS.
I AM THE MATRON OF THIS VILLAGE OF HALF-DEVILS...
CALL ME ELVIRA.
WE'RE SO GLAD TO HAVE YOU WITH US.
PLEASE FORGIVE THE VILLAGERS WHO GREETED YOU ON THE ROAD.
THEY SHOULDN'T HAVE STARTLED YOU LIKE THAT.
TER-RIBLY SORRY.
IT'S OKAY.

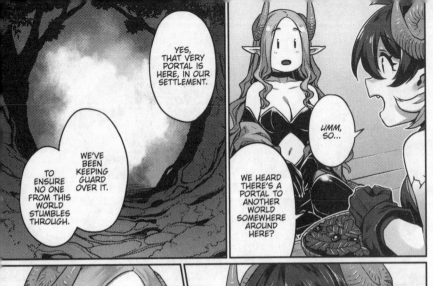

YES, THAT VERY PORTAL IS HERE, IN OUR SETTLEMENT.

WE'VE BEEN KEEPING GUARD OVER IT.

TO ENSURE NO ONE FROM THIS WORLD STUMBLES THROUGH.

UMM, SO...

WE HEARD THERE'S A PORTAL TO ANOTHER WORLD SOMEWHERE AROUND HERE?

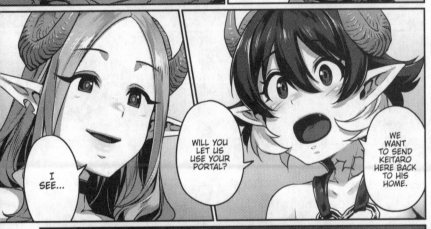

I SEE...

WILL YOU LET US USE YOUR PORTAL?

WE WANT TO SEND KEITARO HERE BACK TO HIS HOME.

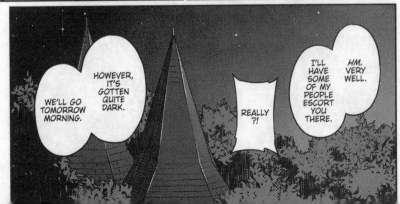

WE'LL GO TOMORROW MORNING.

HOWEVER, IT'S GOTTEN QUITE DARK.

REALLY?!

I'LL HAVE SOME OF MY PEOPLE ESCORT YOU THERE.

HM, VERY WELL.

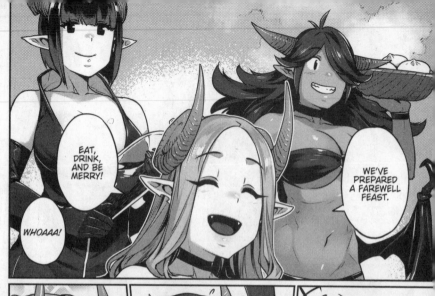

EAT, DRINK, AND BE MERRY!

WHOAAA!

WE'VE PREPARED A FAREWELL FEAST.

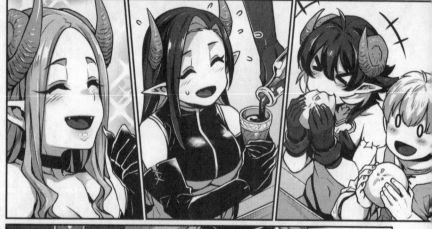

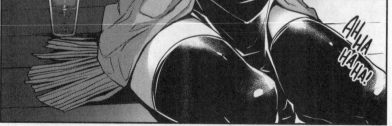

AHHA HAHA!

DIZZY...
HEY, KEITARO.
YOU'RE LOOKING A LITTLE RED. YOU OKAY?
WOBBLE
I DUNNO WHY...
BUT I'M KINDA WOOZY.
WOBBLE
YOU MUST BE TIRED FROM YOUR JOURNEY.
TUG
I'VE PREPARED A ROOM FOR YOU. IT'S JUST THIS WAY...
WE'LL COME ALONG!
THE CHIEFTESS WILL TAKE CARE OF HIM.
DON'T YOU WORRY!
?!

IT'S BEEN A WHILE SINCE WE'VE SEEN OTHER HALF-DEVILS.
TELL ME ALL ABOUT YOUR TRAVELS!
AND THERE'S PLENTY OF FOOD LEFT!
...
JUST RELAX A BIT, HE'LL BE BACK SOON!
UNTIL THEN...
WHAT A HAPPY LITTLE ACCIDENT. ♡
A LOST HUMAN, WANDERING INTO OUR HUMBLE VILLAGE?

THANK YOU FOR ARRIVING BEFORE MY TIME ON THIS WORLD ENDED... KEITARO. ♡
SLIP
LET'S GET RIGHT TO IT...
AND PUT SOME BUNS IN MY OVEN. ♡
CREAK
STROKE

KEITARO SURE IS TAKING A WHILE.
I HOPE HE'S OKAY.
I'M SURE HE'S FINE. OUR MATRIARCH IS WITH HIM.
SURE, BUT I'M STILL WORRIED!
WHY DON'T YOU HAVE A CALMING CUP OF TEA?
NO, THANKS!
LET'S GO CHECK ON HIM.
C'MON, ROSIE!
RGH!
CLENCH
WHAP!

I'M SORRY...
BUT I CAN'T LET YOU IN THAT ROOM!
KRRRR
KRRRR
KRRRRR
FOR THE SAKE...
OF THE CHIEFTESS AND OUR PEOPLE!
HAH! ♡
SLRP
SLRP
MMN! ♡
MNH! ♡
SMOOCH
NN! ♡
SMOOCH

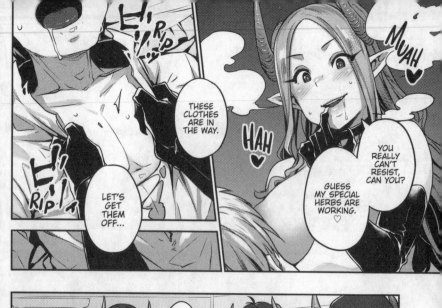

THESE CLOTHES ARE IN THE WAY.

LET'S GET THEM OFF...

MUAH ♥

HAH ♥

YOU REALLY CAN'T RESIST, CAN YOU?

GUESS MY SPECIAL HERBS ARE WORKING. ♥

RIP

RIP

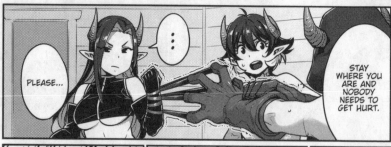

PLEASE...

...

STAY WHERE YOU ARE AND NOBODY NEEDS TO GET HURT.

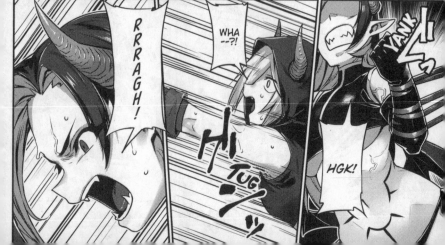

RRRAGH!

WHA--?!

YANK

HI TUG

HGK!

WHI-
RRRRRRRRRRAGHH!!

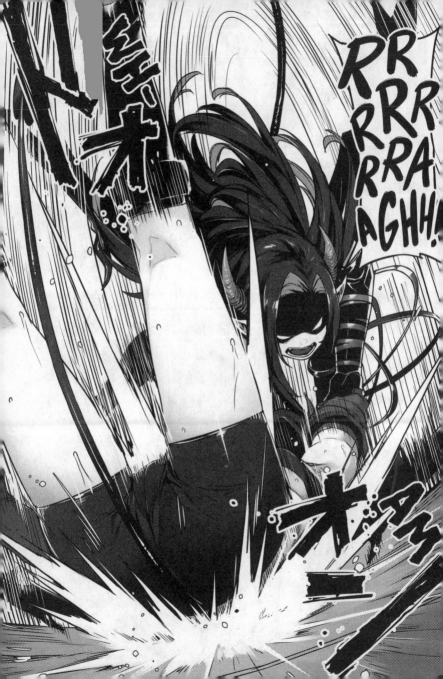

SORRY, BUT I'M NOT GONNA STAY QUIET...
WHILE KEITARO IS IN TROUBLE!
DIZZY
DASH
NIA, LET'S GO!
GOT IT!
HM?
WHUNK
WHOA!
HRGH!
BAM

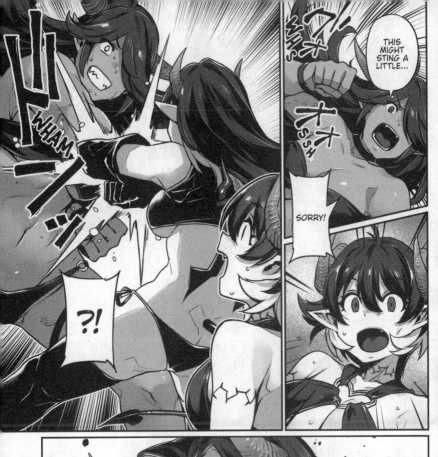

THIS MIGHT STING A LITTLE...

SORRY!

?!

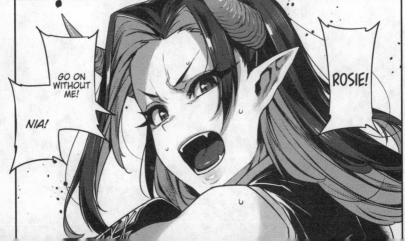

GO ON WITHOUT ME!

NIA!

ROSIE!

CRACK
HOLD I--
WHAT ?!
STRAIN
I WON'T...
LET YOU GO.
KRR
KRR
KRR

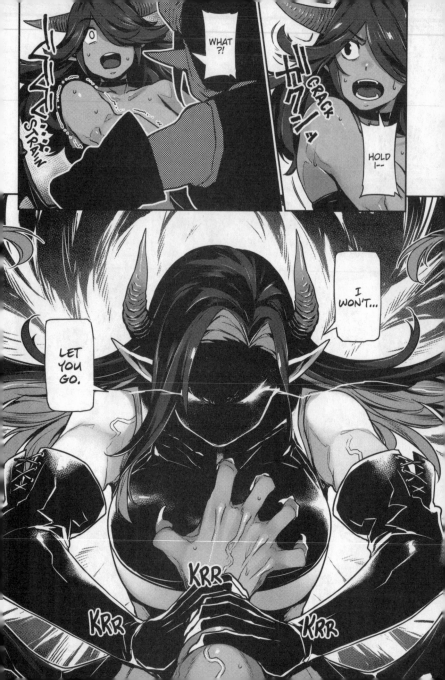

CRACKLE
CRACKLE
CRACKLE
AH...
IT FEELS SOOO MUCH BETTER SKIN-TO-SKIN, DOESN'T IT? MM, KEITARO? ♡
HAH! ♥
HAH! ♥
GH...
JUST RELAX...
LICK
LICK
LET ME TAKE CARE OF YOU. ♡
AH...
TWITCH
TWITCH
FOOOOM!
TWITCH
HAAH...
!

...
GH...
...!
AH!
IT'S OKAY.
DON'T YOU WORRY ABOUT A THING. ♡
HAHH!
HAHH!
HAHH!
!
THERE YOU ARE!

YOU CAN'T COME IN HERE!
THEN I'LL FORCE MY WAY THROUGH!
VERY WELL...
KII!!
COME AT ME!
LEAP

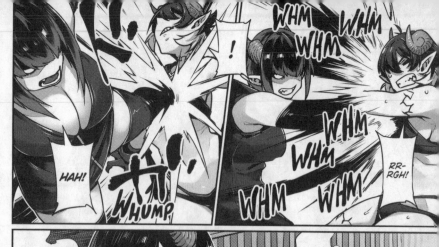

HAH!

WHM WHM WHM WHM

WHM WHM WHM WHM

WHUMP

!

RR-RGH!

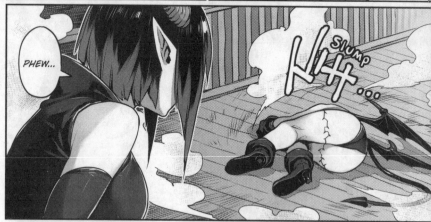

PHEW...

SLUMP...

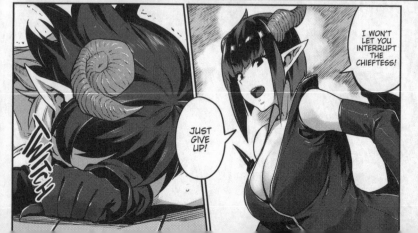

TWITCH

JUST GIVE UP!

I WON'T LET YOU INTERRUPT THE CHIEFTESS!

DID YOU REALLY THINK...
I'D GIVE UP...
AFTER THAT?!

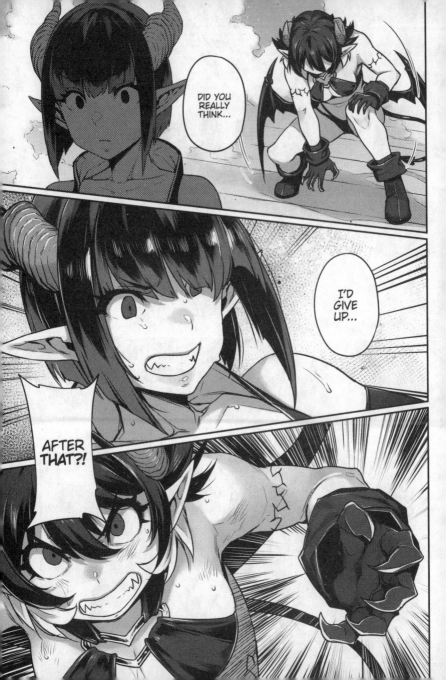

RRRRRRRRAGH!
CRUNCH
CRUMBLE
CRUMBLE
CRUMBLE
HAAH!
KEITARO!
HAAH!
KEITARO, WHERE ARE YOU?!
WSSSHHH

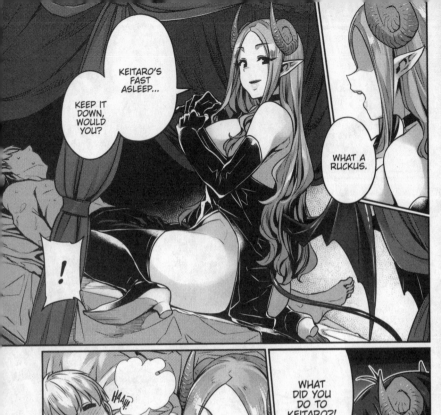

KEITARO'S FAST ASLEEP...

KEEP IT DOWN, WOULD YOU?

WHAT A RUCKUS.

!

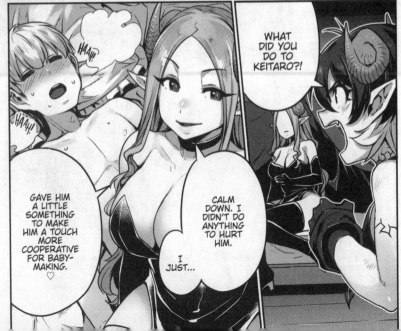

HAAH!

HAAH!

WHAT DID YOU DO TO KEITARO?!

GAVE HIM A LITTLE SOMETHING TO MAKE HIM A TOUCH MORE COOPERATIVE FOR BABY-MAKING. ♡

CALM DOWN. I DIDN'T DO ANYTHING TO HURT HIM.

I JUST...

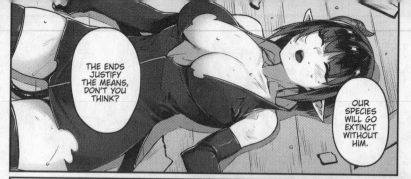

THE ENDS JUSTIFY THE MEANS, DON'T YOU THINK?

OUR SPECIES WILL GO EXTINCT WITHOUT HIM.

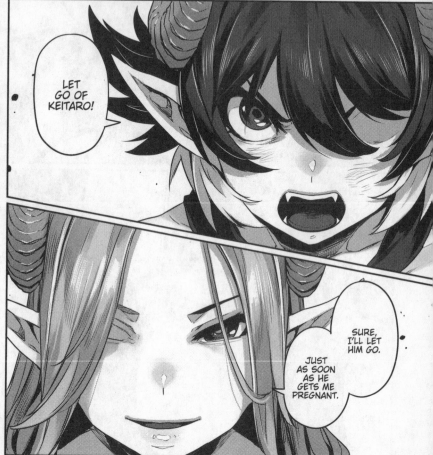

LET GO OF KEITARO!

SURE, I'LL LET HIM GO.

JUST AS SOON AS HE GETS ME PREGNANT.

DEVILISH
DARLINGS
PORTAL
FANTASY

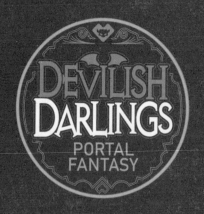

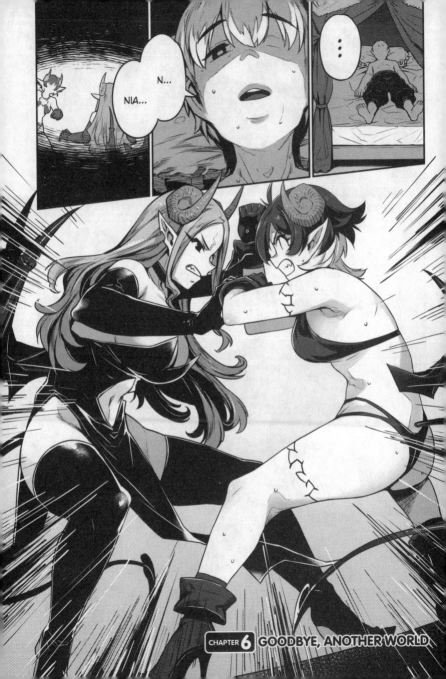

CHAPTER 6 GOODBYE, ANOTHER WORLD

WHM
HAAAAH!
WHM
...!
WHM
WHM
YOUR STRENGTH...
WON'T BE ENOUGH!
YOU WON'T TAKE HIM FROM ME!
WHUNK
I'M FIGHTING FOR OUR FUTURE!

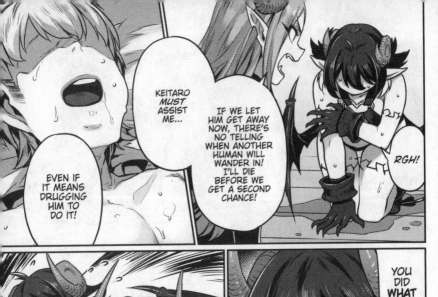

KEITARO MUST ASSIST ME...

IF WE LET HIM GET AWAY NOW, THERE'S NO TELLING WHEN ANOTHER HUMAN WILL WANDER IN! I'LL DIE BEFORE WE GET A SECOND CHANCE!

RGH!

EVEN IF IT MEANS DRUGGING HIM TO DO IT!

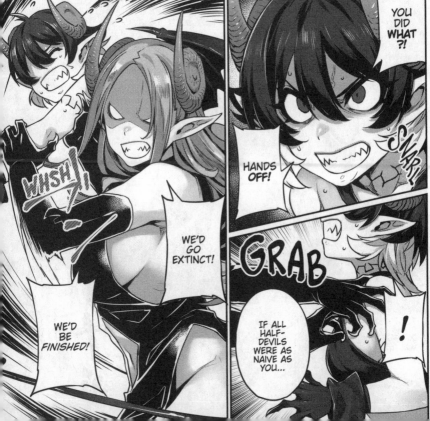

YOU DID WHAT?!

HANDS OFF!

SNARL

WHSH

WE'D GO EXTINCT!

WE'D BE FINISHED!

GRAB

IF ALL HALF-DEVILS WERE AS NAIVE AS YOU...

!

GWAH!
WHAM
RGH...
SLUMP
IF THE HUMAN GOES BACK TO HIS WORLD...
WE MAY NEVER SEE ANOTHER WILLING MAN IN OUR LIFETIMES!
ARE YOU SAYING YOU'RE HAPPY JUST LETTING US DIE OUT?!
I KNOW JUST HOW IMPORTANT KEITARO IS...
TO US HALF-DEVILS!
THEN WHY--
SHUDDER
SHUDDER
THAT DOESN'T MATTER!

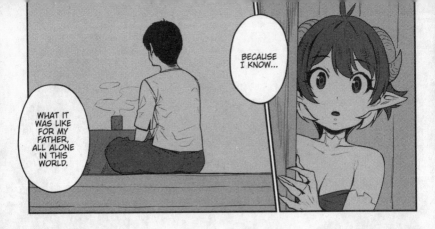

BECAUSE I KNOW...

WHAT IT WAS LIKE FOR MY FATHER, ALL ALONE IN THIS WORLD.

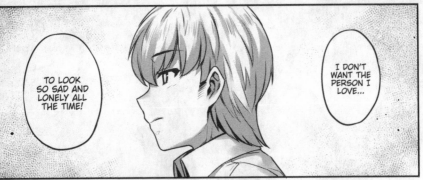

TO LOOK SO SAD AND LONELY ALL THE TIME!

I DON'T WANT THE PERSON I LOVE...

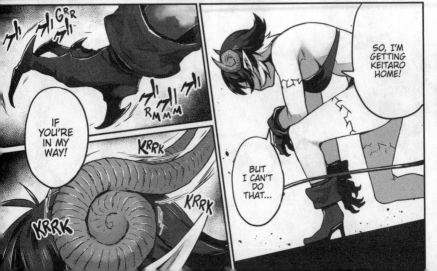

GRR

RMMM

KRRK

IF YOU'RE IN MY WAY!

KRRK

KRRK

SO, I'M GETTING KEITARO HOME!

BUT I CAN'T DO THAT...

WHAT?! THAT FORM...
IT'S LIKE A TRUE DEVIL'S!
HOW CAN SHE DO THIS...?!

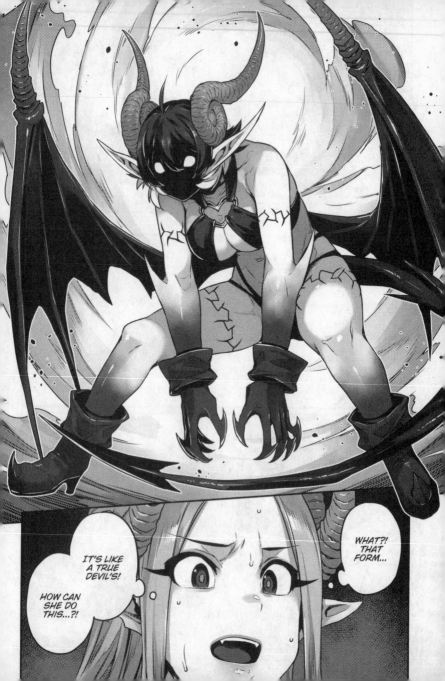

STILL...
I BET YOU'RE ALL SHOW!
BE A GOOD GIRL AND SETTLE DOWN!
CRACK
HUH?!
GLARE
SHUDDER
SLASH
NO!
DODGE

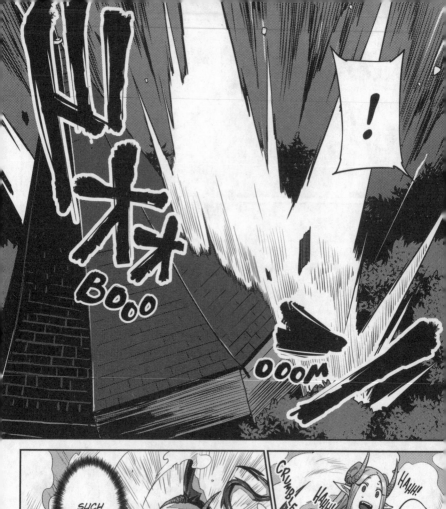

BOOO

OOOM

SUCH POWER...!

THAT WAS FAR TOO CLOSE...

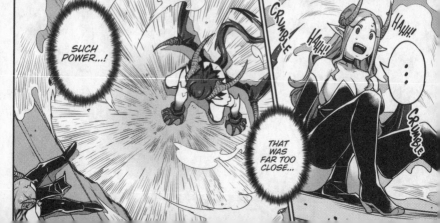

CRUMBLE

HAHH! HAHH! HAHH!

...

CRUMBLE

WHAT ELSE CAN I DO?!
THIS IS THE ONLY WAY TO GET HIM TO AGREE!
YOU'LL UNDERSTAND HOW I FEEL WHEN *YOUR* LIFE IS NEARING ITS END!
SO PLEASE...
GRRRRRRRRRRRRRRRR
EEK!
!

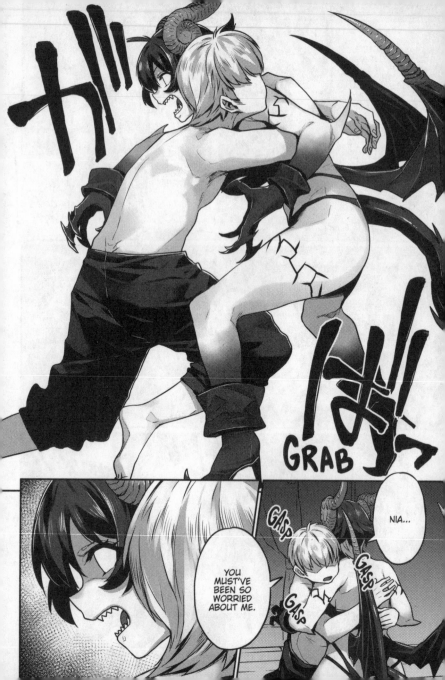

GRAB

NIA...

YOU MUST'VE BEEN SO WORRIED ABOUT ME.

GASP

GASP

GASP

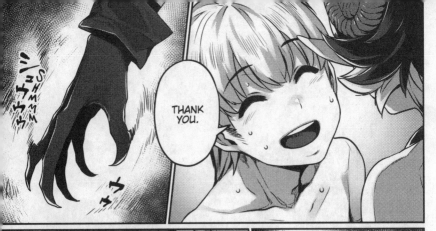

THANK YOU.

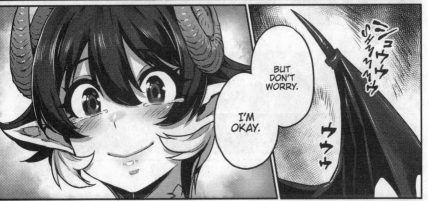

BUT DON'T WORRY.

I'M OKAY.

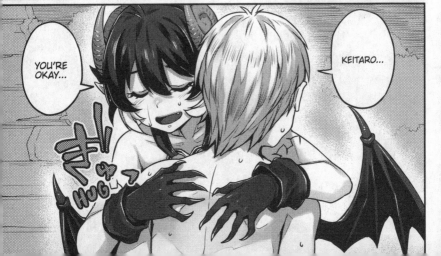

YOU'RE OKAY...

KEITARO...

HUG

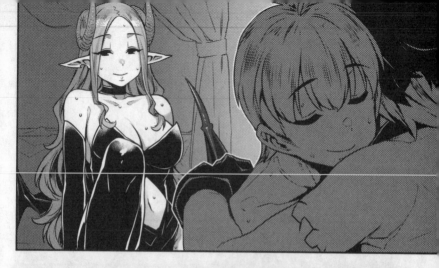

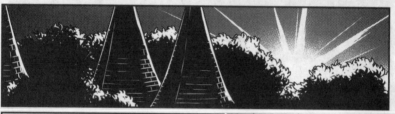

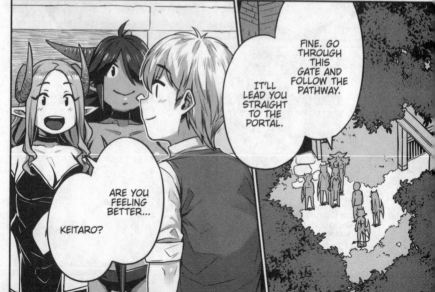

FINE. GO THROUGH THIS GATE AND FOLLOW THE PATHWAY.

IT'LL LEAD YOU STRAIGHT TO THE PORTAL.

ARE YOU FEELING BETTER...

KEITARO?

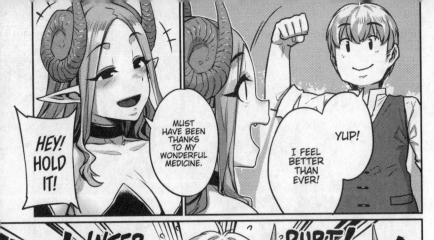

HEY! HOLD IT!

MUST HAVE BEEN THANKS TO MY WONDERFUL MEDICINE.

I FEEL BETTER THAN EVER!

YUP!

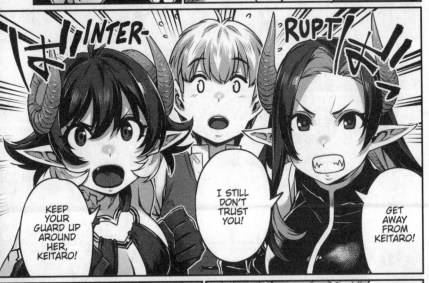

INTER-RUPT!

KEEP YOUR GUARD UP AROUND HER, KEITARO!

I STILL DON'T TRUST YOU!

GET AWAY FROM KEITARO!

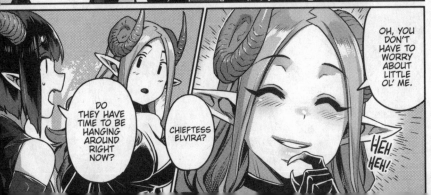

DO THEY HAVE TIME TO BE HANGING AROUND RIGHT NOW?

CHIEFTESS ELVIRA?

OH, YOU DON'T HAVE TO WORRY ABOUT LITTLE OL' ME.

HEH HEH!

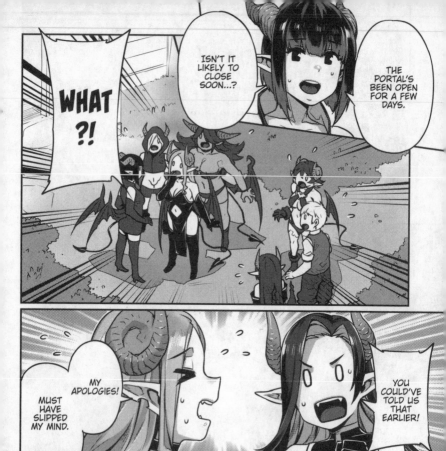

WHAT?!

ISN'T IT LIKELY TO CLOSE SOON...?

THE PORTAL'S BEEN OPEN FOR A FEW DAYS.

MY APOLOGIES! MUST HAVE SLIPPED MY MIND.

YOU COULD'VE TOLD US THAT EARLIER!

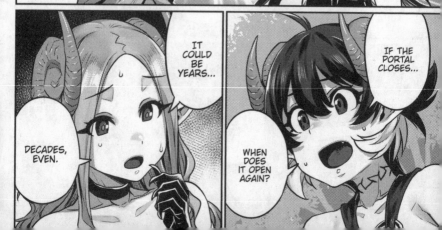

IT COULD BE YEARS...

DECADES, EVEN.

IF THE PORTAL CLOSES...

WHEN DOES IT OPEN AGAIN?

LET'S HURRY!
RIGHT!
KEITARO?
NO ONE HAS PASSED THROUGH THAT PORTAL FROM THIS SIDE YET...
I DO HOPE YOU'LL BE SAFE.
Squeeze
PERHAPS I'LL SEE YOU AGAIN SOMEDAY.
DO DROP IN!
THANKS!

HAAH!
HAAH!
HAAH!
KEI-TARO!
LOOK!
THE PORTAL TO YOUR WORLD!
HAHH!
WE FOUND IT!
HAHH!
BUT IT'S CLOSING!
KEITARO, HURRY!
KSHHH...

AH...
ROSETTE.
NIA.
THANK YOU...
FOR EVERYTHING!

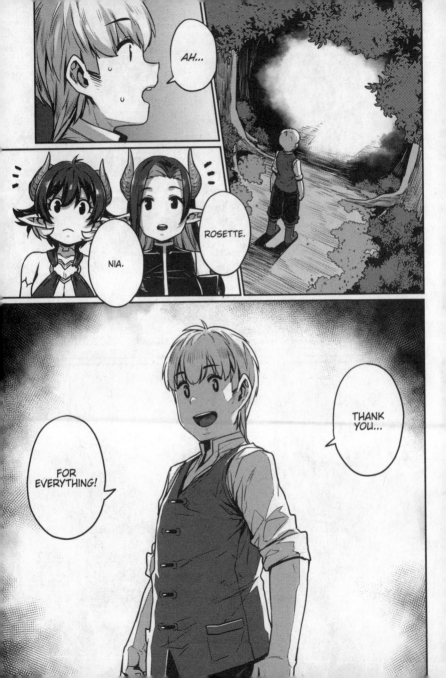

THANK *YOU*, KEITARO!
I HAD SO MUCH FUN!
I'LL NEVER FORGET YOU!
OR THE TIME WE SPENT TOGETHER!
I'LL NEVER FORGET YOU TWO, EITHER!
FAREWELL!

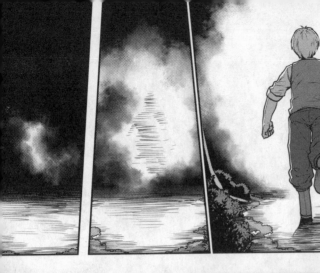

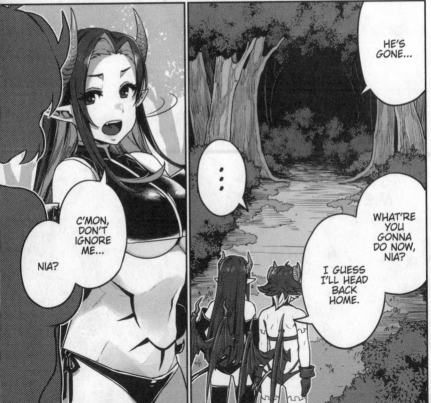

HE'S GONE...

...

WHAT'RE YOU GONNA DO NOW, NIA?

I GUESS I'LL HEAD BACK HOME.

C'MON, DON'T IGNORE ME...

NIA?

SNFF
SNIFFLE
I'M GONNA MISS HIM...

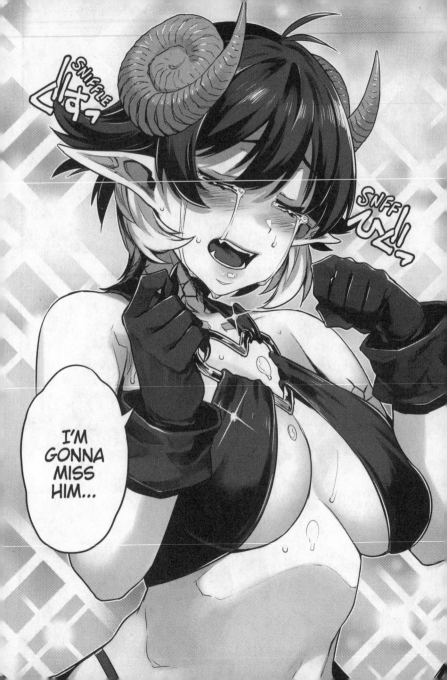

NIA...
HIC... SNIFFLE...
YOU WERE WITH HIM THIS WHOLE TIME.
OF COURSE YOU'RE GONNA MISS HIM.
C'MON, STOP CRYING...
NIA.
YOU'RE CRYING TOO, ROSIE!

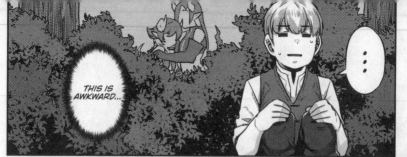

THIS IS AWKWARD...

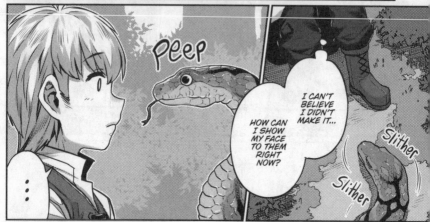

Peep

I CAN'T BELIEVE I DIDN'T MAKE IT...

HOW CAN I SHOW MY FACE TO THEM RIGHT NOW?

Slither

Slither

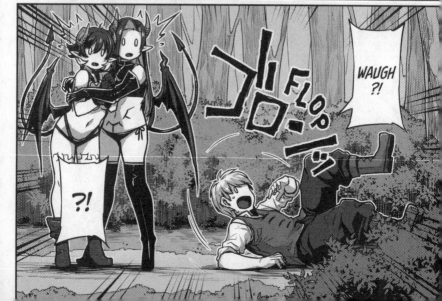

?!

コロ FLOP

WAUGH ?!

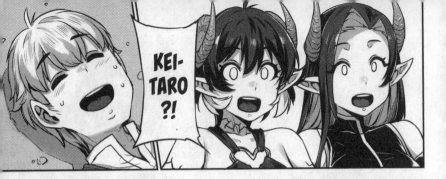

KEI-
TARO
?!

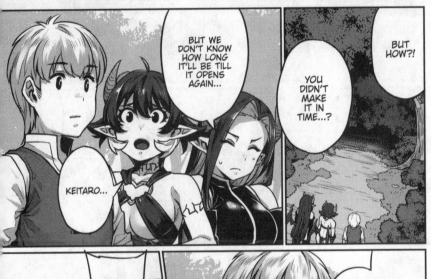

BUT WE DON'T KNOW HOW LONG IT'LL BE TILL IT OPENS AGAIN...

YOU DIDN'T MAKE IT IN TIME...?

BUT HOW?!

KEITARO...

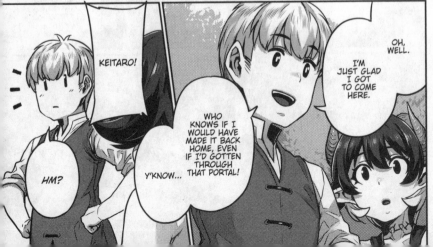

KEITARO!

HM?

WHO KNOWS IF I WOULD HAVE MADE IT BACK HOME, EVEN IF I'D GOTTEN THROUGH THAT PORTAL!

Y'KNOW...

I'M JUST GLAD I GOT TO COME HERE.

OH, WELL.

THE WORLD'S HUGE!
THERE ARE TONS OF PLACES WE'VE NEVER VISITED!
SO, DON'T GIVE UP HOPE JUST YET!
SHE'S RIGHT.
THERE COULD EVEN BE MORE PORTALS TO YOUR WORLD ELSEWHERE IN OURS.
THAT'S RIGHT!
WE'LL JUST HAVE TO TRAVEL THE WHOLE WORLD...
UNTIL WE FIND YOUR HOME!

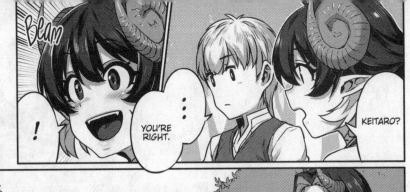

Beam

!

YOU'RE RIGHT.

...

KEITARO?

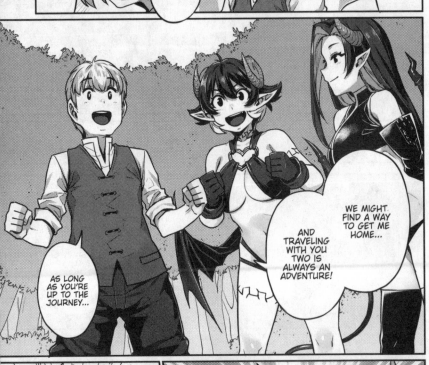

AS LONG AS YOU'RE UP TO THE JOURNEY...

AND TRAVELING WITH YOU TWO IS ALWAYS AN ADVENTURE!

WE MIGHT FIND A WAY TO GET ME HOME...

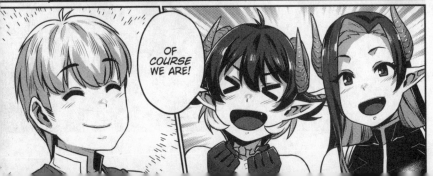

OF COURSE WE ARE!

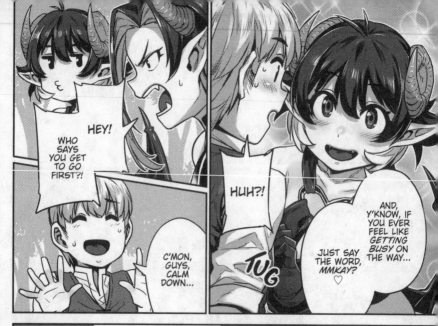

HEY! WHO SAYS YOU GET TO GO FIRST?!

C'MON, GUYS, CALM DOWN...

HUH?!

JUST SAY THE WORD, MMKAY?

AND, Y'KNOW, IF YOU EVER FEEL LIKE *GETTING BUSY* ON THE WAY... ♡

TUG

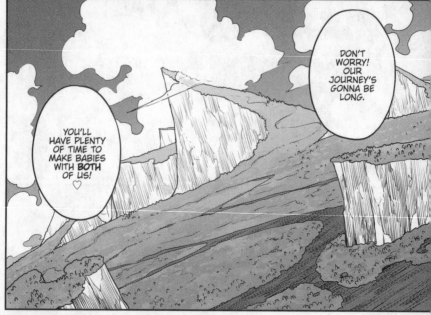

DON'T WORRY! OUR JOURNEY'S GONNA BE LONG.

YOU'LL HAVE PLENTY OF TIME TO MAKE BABIES WITH **BOTH** OF US! ♡